THE WORD OF LIFE

William Challis was Rector of a Bristol Parish for seven years before taking up his current appointment as Vice-Principal of Wycliffe Hall, Oxford, where he teaches Pastoral Studies, Mission and Greek. He is a member of the General Synod of the Church of England. He has also worked as a mission partner in Burundi, training pastors for the Anglican Church, worked in parishes in inner-city London and deepest suburban Bristol, and studied theology in Oxford, London, Rome and Cardiff. He has a wife and two daughters, who tolerate his choice of classical music (which tends towards the operatic), and ignore completely his passion for sport, which nowadays expresses itself in spectating only!

'William Challis brings together much theological wisdom and much pastoral insight into a book that will be a major resource for clergy and ministerial students. In a clear and accessible way, he discusses various central pastoral themes: preaching, counselling, biblical interpretation; and, skilfully negotiating a number of minefields, offers the reader a most helpful map of the territory.'

Canon David Atkinson

D0907456

Other titles available in the Handbooks of Pastoral Care Series

GROWING THROUGH LOSS AND GRIEF
Althea Pearson

COUNSELLING IN CONTEXT
Francis Bridger and David Atkinson

FREE TO LOVE
Margaret Gill

FOR BETTER, FOR WORSE
Bruce and Mary Reddrop

HAPPY FAMILIES?
John and Olive Drane

SETTING CAPTIVES FREE
Bruce Stevens

THE PASTORAL ENCOUNTER
Brice Avery

THE DIVIDED SELF
Marlene Cohen

WORK WELL: LIVE WELL
David Westcott

HANDBOOKS OF PASTORAL CARE
SERIES EDITOR: MARLENE COHEN

THE WORD OF LIFE

Using the Bible in pastoral care

WILLIAM CHALLIS

Marshall Pickering
An Imprint of HarperCollinsPublishers

Marshall Pickering is an Imprint of
HarperCollins*Religious*
Part of HarperCollins*Publishers*
77–85 Fulham Palace Road, London W6 8JB

First published in Great Britain
in 1997 by Marshall Pickering

1 3 5 7 9 10 8 6 4 2

Text Copyright © 1997 William Challis
Introduction Copyright © 1994 Marlene Cohen

William Challis asserts the moral right
to be identified as the author of this work

A catalogue record for this book is
available from the British Library

ISBN 0 551 030615

Printed and bound in Great Britain by
Caledonian International Book Manufacturing Ltd, Glasgow

FOR MELANIE

CONTENTS

Foreword by Alister McGrath   ix

Series Introduction   xi

Preface   xv

Part One — The Pastoral Bible   1
  The Bible as Pastoral Resource; The Bible as Foundation;
  Foundation Stones; The Bible as Focus; The Bible as
  Interpreter; The Bible in Discipline; The Bible in Ethics;
  The Bible in Worship; The Bible in Counselling;
  Towards a Pastoral Hermeneutic of Scripture;
  The True Interpreter

Part Two — Proclaiming the Pastoral Word
1. Preaching and Pastoral Care   29
2. Pastoral Preaching in Practice   39
3. Counselling and Proclamation   56
4. Truth is Pastoral   65

Part Three — Expounding the Pastoral Word
1. Paul the Pastor — Perspectives on Pastoral Theology
   from the Corinthian Epistles   79
2. God the Pastor — The Book of Jeremiah as
   Pastoral Theology   93

Part Four — Evangelical Pastoral Writers and the Bible
1. Jay Adams' *More than Redemption* — The Bible as Textbook   126
2. Lawrence Crabb's *Understanding People* — The Bible as
   Framework   146
3. Roger Hurding's *Roots and Shoots* — The Bible as Touchstone   156
4. Derek Tidball's *Skilful Shepherds* — The Bible as Foundation   162

Epilogue — Towards an Evangelical Pastoral Theology   169
Suggestions for Further Reading   173
Index of Scripture References   177
Index by Author and Subject   183

FOREWORD

One of the most encouraging trends in today's Church is the increasing thought being given to pastoral ministry. More and more pastors are concerned to ensure that their ministry is thoroughly grounded in Scripture, not simply in terms of what they preach and teach, but in terms of the way in which they conduct their pastoral ministry.

In this lucid and stimulating book, William Challis lays out a careful and clear analysis of the questions which must be answered in the course of developing authentically biblical approaches to ministry. It is clear that this book has emerged from a deep passion to minister faithfully to the people of God, informed by an awareness of the biblical resources and the increasingly important discipline of pastoral theology. Many will find the interaction with four leading representatives of evangelical pastoral theology particularly helpful in clarifying their own thinking on this important issue.

Many have found earlier efforts to explore the role of the Bible in pastoral care unappealing, on account of their dreary and confusing technical vocabulary, their failure to be grounded properly in Scripture, or an absence of pastoral experience on the part of their authors. This book avoids those fatal weaknesses, and is set to become a major resource for this wishing to think in a biblical and relevant way about pastoral care. I warmly recommend this book and the freshness of its approach to this important aspect of modern Church life.

Alister E. McGrath
Principal, Wycliffe Hall

SERIES INTRODUCTION

The demand for pastoral care and counselling in churches has increased to record levels and every indication is that this trend will continue to accelerate. Some churches are fortunate to have ready access to professionally trained and qualified counsellors, but in most situations this onerous task falls to pastors.

Some pastors* are naturally gifted for the ministry of counselling. Some receive training before ordination and then seek to extend this as opportunity permits through the years. Others have the task of counselling thrust upon them. Most seem to feel some sustained demand, internal or external, to be competent in the field. This series aims to address some of the gaps frequently left in theological training. It is intended to offer support to those entrusted with responsibility for the care and well-being of others.

Comparative studies of healing agencies were pioneered in the United States. As long as thirty years ago The Joint Commission on Mental Illness reported that forty per cent of 2,460 people canvassed would go first to the clergy with any mental health problem.

Of course there may be reasons other than overtly religious ones for a preference for clergy counselling. There may seem less stigma in seeing a pastor than a psychiatrist. Also, viewing a problem as a primarily spiritual matter may preclude taking some degree of

*The term 'pastor' is used generically here, to include all who have a recognized pastoral role within a local church or Christian community.

responsibility for it and for examining its depths. And, of course, clergy visits are cheaper! Unfortunately, there can be the additional reason that parishioners feel an inappropriate right of access to their pastor's time and skills. God's availability at all times is sometimes confused with ours, as is divine omniscience.

Being a front-line mental health worker can put a pastor under enormous and inappropriate strain. Counselling is becoming the primary time consumer in an increasing number of parish ministries.

Feeling unsafe and inadequate in any situation inevitably produces some form of self-protective behaviour, unless we can admit our inadequacy while retaining self-respect. Religious professionals who are under pressure to function as counsellors, but know their skills and knowledge to be in other areas, may understandably take refuge in various defences, even dogmatism. The term 'religious professional' is more familiar in some countries than in others. The clerical profession actually preceded all others, in status and in time. 'But what are we professional at?' can be a difficult question to answer. This is especially so when clergy are driven to believe that anything short of multi-competence will let God down.

Pastors may feel obliged not to appear inadequate in the area of counselling because of their confidence that the Bible contains the answer to every human need. And it does, conceptually. The difficulty is not with the Bible nor with the pastor's knowledge of the Bible. Neither of these should be in question. The concern is whether pastors have the additional ability of a clinician. Naming a counselling problem correctly – not the presenting problem but the real, underlying issues and their components – is a refined specialism. Making a faulty diagnosis, especially when God and biblical authority are somehow implicated, is the cause of much damage. Clinical terminology can be applied almost at random but with a surprising degree of assurance. Understanding the Bible, and understanding the complexities of clinical practice, are not one and the same skill. In 1985 a comparative study was conducted into the ability of 112 clergy to recognize 13 signs of suicidal tendencies. (Reported in the *Journal of Psychology and Theology*, 1989, Vol 17, No. 2.) It was found that clergy were unable to recognize these signs any better than educated lay people and substantially less well than other mental health workers. This is no necessary reflection on the clergy. Why should they be expected to have this professional ability? Considering them culpable would only be just if they were to assume, or to allow an assumption to go unchecked, that their skills were identical to those of other caring professionals.

One pressure is that graduates of some theological colleges have actually been taught that ordination will confer counselling skills. 'We must insist upon the idea that every man who has been called of God into the ministry has been given the basic gifts for ... counselling' (Jay Adams, *The Christian Counsellor's Manual*, 1973, Presbyterian and Reformed Publishing Company, Part One, page 20).

Equating a ministry calling with being a gifted counsellor could be seen to involve some leaping assumptions. These are becoming more apparent as we distinguish what we used to call 'the ministry' from God's calling of *all* believers into ministry. As more work is done on what we mean by 'ordination' more clergy can be released into those areas of ministry for which they are clearly gifted and suited.

Belief that counselling skills are divinely bestowed in conjunction with a ministry 'call' will probably not issue in the purchase of this series of handbooks! Other pastors who believe or fear that neither counselling nor any other skills can be taken for granted, are possibly conducting their ministries under some heavy burdens. This series is written with a concern to address these burdens and to redress some erroneous equations that relate to them. Each author has extensive experience in some avenue of ministry and is also trained and experienced in some aspect of counselling.

These Handbooks of Pastoral Care are designed to aid pastors in assessing the needs of those who come to them for help. The more accurately this assessment can be made the more confident the pastor can be about the form of ministry that is required in each instance. Sometimes pastors will decide to refer the matter elsewhere, but on other occasions there can be a prayerful assurance in retaining the counselling role within their own ministry.

Marlene Cohen
Oxford, March 1994

PREFACE

The aim of this book is modest, but it springs from a profound concern, which I believe is shared by many involved in Christian ministry. This concern is for the Bible. I desire that its authority be recognized and worked out in my ministry. The Bible is the Word of God, it is the only testimony to Jesus Christ, it is the work of the inspiring Holy Spirit. This belief is, in my understanding, the only belief consistent with historic Christian teaching. My concern is also for pastoral ministry. It is this ministry to which the Bible itself points. It is to this ministry that I myself have been called. I do not find it difficult to give assent to the statement that 'Holy Scripture containeth all things necessary to salvation', nor to answer the question 'Do you think in your heart that you be truly called ... to the Order and Ministry of Priesthood?', both of which are required of all those ordained in my own denomination, the Church of England.[1] I do, however, become increasingly aware of the inadequacies of my own understanding of the Scriptures and of the awesome responsibility of pastoral ministry as the years go on. If my understanding of the authority of the Bible and my understanding of the importance of pastoral ministry are both true, they must belong together, the one must intimately interact with and affect the other, because both the Scriptures and the ministry come from the same God.

How many of us truly hold together the authority of the Bible and the experience of pastoral ministry? Those involved in pastoral ministry, whether ordained or lay, tend to fall into one of three categories. Some have lost all confidence in the Bible. They have seen their faith in it leak away through the ever-widening cracks created by a corrosive liberal theology, offered, and frequently accepted quite uncritically, from pulpit and lecture room. Frankly they have rejected the Bible as having any important part to play in their ministry. Others acknowledge clearly and with conviction the authority of Scripture. It is their constant companion in the pulpit, they delight to expound it Sunday by Sunday. But it plays little or no part in their ministry the rest of the week. In their pastoral encounters with individuals or groups they rely more on native wit or on insights gained from other secular disciplines to see them through. Their ministry is not so impoverished as that of the first group, but it is quite often marred by an inconsistency, of which the minister may very well be quite unconscious. The third group is equally sure of the authority of the Scriptures, and of their visible role in pastoral ministry. The Bible goes with them everywhere. No encounter can be deemed to have been handled in a Christian way unless the Bible has been explicitly opened and quoted. Some in this group may indeed have very few pastoral encounters, because they see their ministry as consisting solely of 'preaching and teaching'. They spend their weekdays in their studies, and a large part of their Sundays in their pulpits.

I suggest that all three of these styles of ministry are inadequate. The first is barely Christian, the last barely human. The one fails to offer people anything that truly speaks of God and contains no element of transformation in Christ. The other can seem irrelevant, or indeed crass and insensitive. The second style of ministry is more complex to assess, but it is clearly dualistic. There are probably many of us who have managed to maintain such a style of ministry over many years, but further reflection, and pastoral practice, make it appear increasingly unsatisfactory.

My concern, therefore, is that Bible and pastoral ministry belong together. They are not to be set in opposition — conscious or unconscious — to each other, but to be integrated. The authority of the Bible must be worked out in practice, not just in theory. The reality of pastoral experience must be allowed to meet our biblical understanding. The aim of this book is to try to encourage those called to pastoral ministry to think about how that integration can be accomplished, how our ministry can be truly biblical and truly pastoral. This is not a question that has been much addressed in . modern pastoral theology, perhaps because of an almost complete failure on the part of evangelical theologians to contribute to pastoral thinking for most of the twentieth century. There is no great corpus of literature on the subject for me to refer to. This book, therefore, cannot claim to provide definitive answers. All it can do is to raise questions and point to possible lines of enquiry that might prove fruitful to pursue.

I shall feel that my aims have been achieved if others take up some of these questions, if pastors are encouraged by this book to think more biblically, if biblical expositors and theologians are encouraged to think more pastorally.

My thinking of these questions began to develop seriously during a sabbatical from the Diocese of Bristol during the first part of 1991. I was extremely fortunate to be welcomed as an honorary visiting lecturer to the Department of Theology in the University of Wales, College of Cardiff, for those months. Paul Ballard shared his time and wisdom with me with great generosity. My colleagues at Wycliffe Hall, to which I moved at the end of 1992, have also offered me much stimulus and encouragement, especially Vera Sinton, David Atkinson and Alister McGrath. Because the book springs out of my own pastoral experience, many people have contributed to it, in some ways of which I am probably unconscious. There may be statements and ideas referred to in this book which come originally from other people, but which I am now unable to trace back to their source. If any readers recognize their thinking in the pages that follow, I hope they will forgive me for any failure to give appropriate attribution. My thanks go out especially to the people of the parish of Bishopston, Bristol, and to the community of Wycliffe Hall, Oxford, for their willingness to put up with my pastoral ministry amongst them.

It is a great privilege for me to contribute to such a distinguished series as the *Handbooks of Pastoral Care*. I am particularly grateful to the Series Editor, Marlene Cohen, for telling me I had to write a book for the series, and then backing up her orders with constant encouragement, and to Christine Smith and her successors at HarperCollins, especially Kathy Dyke and Philippa Linton, for their continued support.

Whilst all the above deserve much thanks for their help with this book, none of them deserve any blame for the inadequacy of the contents. The responsibility is all mine.

Lastly, may I thank my family for not complaining too much when I have been late home for dinner because it has taken me longer to get out of my elderly word processor than I thought it would.

My God enrich all who read this book in a ministry that is indeed truly biblical and truly pastoral.

William Challis
Feast of St Mark the Evangelist, 1996

Note

1. Article VI and The Ordering of Priests in *The Book of Common Prayer*.

Part One

THE PASTORAL BIBLE

The Bible as Pastoral Resource

It might seem that there is not much for us to explore in the theme of the Pastoral Bible. Perhaps the pastoral importance and role of the Bible seems secure. The pastor naturally takes the Bible into the pulpit on Sunday, the study or nurture group naturally gathers round the Bible for its evening meetings; the pastoral role of the Bible in these situations seems clear, even if its authority is understood in different ways in the various traditions of Christianity. A recent Christian Resources Exhibition in Britain advertised itself as concentrating on the Bible, the supreme Christian resource. But is the Bible seen – and used – as a pastoral resource in the counselling session, in the day-by-day pastoral visiting, in the PCC or church leaders' meeting, in the meeting with local authority representatives to discuss the provision of youth work in the locality? Where is the Bible then? Is it simply carried by the pastor or laid on the table as some sort of symbol of orthodoxy, the 'big, black Bible' of the traditional minister? Even when it is I suspect that what lies between its black covers is often ignored. Why?

Stephen Pattison suggests that it is partly because of the rise of liberal scholarship which has robbed Christians of their former confidence in Scripture, and partly because the Bible does not appear to have very much to say about pastoral care.[1] The latter reason undoubtedly has some truth, as the Bible is emphatically not a handbook of pastoral care. Nevertheless, it is a very superficial reader who concludes that it has nothing to say about it. As we shall see, the Bible offers us a rich variety of themes and images to inform our understanding of the pastoral task.

The former reason may also have some force, but I suspect that even those Christians who still wish to uphold the normative authority of Scripture in a traditional sense are no better at seeing the Bible as a pastoral resource than are more liberal Christians. How many evangelicals, whose tradition readily acknowledges the Bible as supremely authoritative in all matters of faith and conduct, acknowledge the Bible as one of their pastoral resources in the type of practical situations mentioned above?

Perhaps the real reason for the neglect of the Bible in pastoral practice is simply the difficulty of working out *how* it is to be used in pastoral situations. As Oglesby points out in discussing pastoral counselling, translating biblical authority into the manner of conducting a counselling conversation 'is complex indeed'.[2] But should that complexity make us run away from attempting to find some answers to this problem? It certainly appears to have caused paralysis amongst the pastoral theologians. Stephen Pattison perhaps overstates the case when he says that there is 'no significant British work in the use of the Bible in pastoral care',[3] because writers such as Lambourne, Lake and Hurding have tried to address the question from the viewpoint of various traditions; their contributions may certainly be regarded as significant, although none has produced a major work on the subject. But surely, if the Bible is authoritative, however one understands the nature and limits of that authority, then we must consider how it is authoritative in practice, and not just in theory. If the Bible has no role to play in the Church's pastoral task, then it is difficult to see how we can still claim that it is authoritative. The Bible may not be a handbook of pastoral practice, but it is surely a pastoral resource. We need to consider some of the ways in which it acts as such a resource.

The Bible as Foundation

To say that the Bible is a pastoral resource does not mean to say that it has to be used overtly in pastoral situations, either in a physical fashion or in the constant quotation of texts.

The Bible is present as the foundation on which the Christian pastor, whoever that person may be, builds his or her work. In a building, foundations are hidden, but they are vital. In any professional task, it is necessary to have the right foundations; the doctor does not refer to a textbook every time a patient attends for a consultation, but the knowledge gained from the appropriate training enables the doctor to set out the right course of treatment for the patient's condition, and we expect our doctors to keep going back to their textbooks, old and new, for further study, to maintain and improve their competence. We take that foundation for granted. One should not give the impression that Christian pastoral work is necessarily equivalent to the work of professional 'experts' such as doctors; much more pastoral care is done by the ordinary members of the Christian community as individuals and as a body, and even the ordained pastor needs to be aware of the dangers of the 'professional' tag, but Christian pastoral work is no less in need of the appropriate foundation than the work of the doctor or solicitor. If pastoral work is to be genuinely Christian it must be thoroughly rooted in the Christian tradition, and the fountainhead of that tradition is the Bible.

Eugene H. Peterson describes the way the American author Annie Dillard uses the Bible:

> She has assimilated Scripture so thoroughly, is so saturated with its cadences and images, that it is simply at hand, unbidden, as context and metaphor for whatever she happens to be writing about. She does not, though, use Scripture to prove or document; it is not a truth she 'uses' but one she lives. Her knowledge of Scripture is stored in her right brain rather than her left; nourishment for the praying imagination rather than fuel for apologetic argument. She seldom quotes Scripture; she alludes constantly. There is scarcely a page that does not contain one or several allusions, but with such nonchalance, not letting her left hand know what her right hand is doing, that someone without a familiarity with Scripture might never notice the biblical precept and story.[4]

Just as the Bible is constantly present for Dillard in her writing, so it is constantly present, even though covertly, for the Church in its pastoral ministry.

Foundation Stones

The Bible acts as the foundation of pastoral work in a variety of ways. Firstly, it sets out *the context of the pastoral task*. The context of Christian pastoral work is not human need, it is God. The biblical record of God as Creator and Redeemer, Lord of the universe and Lover of human beings, provides the context in which to understand human need; the biblical account of human sin, and of God's work in Christ to bring salvation from that sin provides the context in which to understand human nature and aspirations; the biblical vision of a renewed community, the Body of Christ, provides the context in which Christians can live and work out their pastoral call. The Christian pastor will hope to lead the person who comes to speak about an individual problem to the place where that problem can be brought to God. The pastoral task with a congregation is not simply to get them to like each other and work together well, it must involve their growing in worship of the one God, and understanding better his will for their own lives and the life of the world.

Secondly, the Bible sets out *the nature of the pastoral task*. We cannot see that pastoral task in a purely humanistic context, nor can we set its limits according to a purely humanistic agenda. Too often the Church has failed at this very point, and narrowed the pastoral task to limits that are not biblical. The most notable example of this has been the twentieth century's tendency, most marked in American pastoral writing and practice, to limit pastoral care purely to the field of pastoral counselling. This came about partly as a result of a loss of confidence amongst pastors in the traditional Christian equipment and training for the pastoral task. The failure of nerve that ensued led to a search for new, more 'relevant' skills that would enable pastors to take their place in the world of 'professionals'. Whilst much good has come out of this desire for psychotherapeutic training and skills, it has resulted in a neglect of many areas of traditional pastoral work and a tendency for pastoral theology to be reduced to psychology, as well as a reduction of pastoral care to dealing with the 'abnormal'. The Bible's vision of pastoral work is much broader than this; it probably cannot be summed up in one word, but a word regularly used by Paul in the Corinthian epistles, *oikodomein* – 'build up' God's Temple, God's building which is his worshipping, servant people, the Body of Christ – perhaps embraces the broad vision of the pastoral task that emerges from a careful reading of Scripture.

Thirdly, the Bible also sets out *essential images of pastoral care*. It offers us models of pastoral work which reflect God's nature and work. Humanistic models might suggest that pastors are experts or leaders, the Bible will remind us that they are also humble shepherds and suffering servants. The supreme model offered by the Bible is, of course, Jesus Christ himself, who is not only a model for the pastor and the Church's whole pastoral work, but also a model of human wholeness. The Bible therefore operates pastorally by constantly challenging those doing pastoral work to consider whether their manner of operating, their attitudes, are in line with the images it gives us, supremely the images of Jesus Christ. Paul describes the aim of his ministry as being 'that we may present everyone perfect in Christ' (Colossians 1:28); he is the model towards which Christian pastoral concern must aim. The Bible is, in fact, rich in images of the pastoral task and the pastor, some of which we shall consider further in Part Three; that richness is, in itself, an indication of the breadth of a fully biblical picture of pastoral work.[5]

Images of pastoral care in the Bible are found interwoven with theological themes which offer us directions for pastoral work. Oglesby has developed some of these in terms of pastoral counselling to demonstrate how the counsellor and the counsellee can find it fruitful to explore such biblical themes as 'Initiative and Freedom' or 'Risk and Redemption' in counselling conversation.[6] We need to have a style in pastoral work which reflects the biblical pattern, we need to be concerned for the very things that concern the biblical authors. Biblical images, biblical themes, biblical concerns must fashion and direct our pastoral work, and it can be demonstrated that to build on the foundation of these biblical themes is fruitful.

Fourthly, the Bible sets out *the distinctive nature of Christian pastoral care*. As we have already seen, the Church has often fallen prey to the temptation to model its pastoral work on humanistic models rather than to retain confidence in a truly Christian, biblical model of pastoral work. In recent years, however, there has been a strong reaction against this trend in pastoral practice, and pastoral theologians have again been emphasizing the distinctive nature of Christian pastoral care. Clinebell, for instance, points out how much richer the biblical picture of human life is than that offered by humanistic psychology,[7] and goes on to point out also the distinctive nature of Christian ministry: 'The heart of our uniqueness is our theological and pastoral heritage, orientation, resources, and awareness.'[8] The basis of that heritage is, of course, the Bible, and the Christian pastoral tradition shows how the Bible can be used 'growthfully'.[9] The Christian pastor must, of course, be aware of the insights gained by the contemporary human and social sciences, but to attempt to build on a foundation of those sciences rather than on a biblical foundation is to blur the distinctiveness of Christian pastoral ministry. One cannot have a distinctively Christian pastoral ministry, marked by the features set out above, unless it is built on truly Christian foundations. It is the Bible, as the foundation of the whole Christian heritage, which acts also as the foundation of a truly Christian pastoral theology.

The Bible as Focus

The Bible also functions as a focus for the pastoral work of the Christian community. If, in its foundational role, it helps to maintain the distinctively Christian character of pastoral work, so it does in its role as focus, although this function of the Bible does not seem to have been much commented upon by pastoral theologians.

It is not too difficult to discover groups and organized activities which were begun within the Christian community, and originally were conceived with a distinctively Christian purpose in mind, to enable Christian fellowship, nurture or outreach. However, because of a lack of a distinctive Christian focus, these groups no longer fulfil their original pastoral function, and now operate in a more or less secular manner, with no vision of *oikodomia*, which is so essential to

Paul, remaining. The Male Voice Choir of the South Wales valleys is a good example of such a group, as is Everton Football Club, originally founded as a church football team! A much more serious example is an institution such as the Westminster Pastoral Foundation or the YMCA, founded with a distinctly Christian purpose which appears to have been much diluted over the years. On a more local level, many churches still have, loosely attached to them, some kind of group, perhaps a women's meeting or activity group, officially acknowledged as a church group, but no longer with any distinctively Christian character, and no longer effective either in providing real fellowship or nurture for Christians or in reaching out to non-Christians. They have stopped being pastoral communities in any meaningfully Christian sense.

Pastors and church councils frequently comment on the frustrations caused by such groups. Why have these groups lost their Christian character and effectiveness? Perhaps because they have no Christian focus. In a discussion about the home groups in my former parish, one of my colleagues suggested that it would not matter what the groups studied – 'they could even sit round the telephone directory' – what was important was that Christians met together for fellowship. This was countered by the very observation made above, that a group, even if composed of Christians, can lose its distinctively Christian nature and effectiveness if there is no genuinely Christian focus, and the obvious focus for a Christian nurture group is the Bible.

One needs to sound a warning here. The Bible is a focus not in itself, but because of what it points to, the One who is revealed in its pages; it is a channel through which Christ comes to us, and our thoughts and lives are brought to Christ. To describe the Bible as a focus is not to say that it must become a fetish. Protestant tradition has often been as guilty of using the Bible as a fetish as Catholic tradition has been of using statues or some sacramental practices. 'We only stand up when the Bible is carried in to church,' was the complaint of one strict Presbyterian when he realized that the congregation in a church he was visiting had stood at the entry of the ministers. The physical presence of a Bible is no more adequate a focus for the Christian community than any other object. To see the Bible carried under the minister's arm, or to see it laid on the table in the church meeting, does not mean that what is going on here is biblical. To describe the Bible as a foundation and a focus in pastoral practice is to point beyond the physical presence and printed words of the Bible to Christ, who is revealed to us through the Scriptures, and who is the only true, secure foundation for the whole of Christian life (1 Corinthians 3:11).

As I have already said, there seems to be little investigation by pastoral writers of the Bible's function as a focus; my own observations are based entirely on *ad hoc* experience. I suspect some more work needs to be done in this area.

The Bible as Interpreter

'All learning takes place from experience.'[10] That concern for experiential learning seems to be a commonplace of contemporary pastoral theology; the situation must be allowed to speak with its full weight, or an inauthentic theology results. Professor James Poling has described the function of pastoral theology as being to prevent theology becoming oppressive, denying the truth of people's experience. This concern is shared with liberation theologians, for whom 'a hermeneutic which starts from the Bible must be displaced by a new hermeneutic which starts from the world ... any *prior* reference to Scripture can only lead to an irrelevant agenda for theology.'[11] The obvious danger of such an approach, of course, is that one ends up in a sea of subjectivism, which has lost any right to be regarded as authentically Christian. So, given the importance of learning from experience and of recognizing the rightful authority of the current situation, is there a role for the Bible which might help to prevent such a decline into subjectivism? The function of the Bible in learning is, in fact, an interpretative one.

In the course of its pastoral work, the Christian community comes face to face with a situation, perhaps an individual in need, perhaps a need in the wider community, such as an unacceptably high level of unemployment, or a need in the church, large numbers of young people leaving after confirmation or believer's baptism. How is one to understand this situation correctly? Human sciences will undoubtedly help in some ways, a historical perspective will probably offer important information as well, but there must also be a theological perspective on the situation, if we are to understand it in a genuinely Christian way. The pastoral theologian's task, therefore, is to establish a 'conversation', to use a word borrowed from American pastoral literature, between human experience and the Christian tradition.[12] A situation will only be seen in its true light when it is brought into the light of the Christian tradition, the head of which is the Bible, and we need to do the hard work necessary to understand both the situation facing us and the Scriptures which help us to understand it, and to bring those two together.

Laurie Green, writing about ministry in the inner city, also shows how the Bible can be used to interpret the pastoral situation. In his book *Power to the Powerless*,[13] which deals with his experiences in the parish of 'Spaghetti Junction' in Birmingham, Green shows how a group of people, committed to learning from experience, found the pastoral situations facing them constantly illuminated by Jesus' parables. A period of waiting for a new project to be accepted and used could have been frustrating and damaging; those involved were encouraged by the theme of delay in the parables, as well as the frequent references to waiting in the rest of the Bible. 'A biblical parable makes us look upon the world from a totally new and Godward perspective'[14]; parables enable us to discern not only the signs of the Kingdom of God, but also the signs of the times, they help us to interpret our situation correctly. And they take us even further than simple interpretation towards transformation: 'The parable or kingdom sign places the hearers at a new crossroads and calls them to participate in or be judged by the action it symbolizes.'[15]

As Green's group developed their work together, they discovered that it was not only the parables which helped illuminate and interpret their situation; when they were faced with a frustrating period of waiting for a carefully planned project to come to fruition, they were able to find many biblical examples of waiting, the wilderness wanderings, Psalms, prophetic promises, Simeon, Jesus' waiting for the beginning of his ministry, and his temptations.

In his next book, *Let's Do Theology*, Green develops his thinking by setting out a structure which enables this process to happen in a group.[16] His spiral structure of theological learning, which begins with experience, has a central place for reflection.[17] In this reflection, we look for the presence of God in our situation, and bring the Christian tradition alongside our experience. This is vital, he says, because 'in bringing our Christian heritage into connection with our contemporary experience, we guard against a blinkered acceptance of the world.'[18] The Bible will shed light on our situation through similarities, oppositions, or through connections which may come at first just as 'unclear intuitive *hunches* or suspicions'.[19] Green is totally committed to the concept of experiential learning, starting the learning process from our contemporary experience, but, as he says, 'while theological reflection may ... follow on after the experience and exploration phases, it only comes after in terms of methodology, whereas in terms of importance, it precedes them both.'[20]

In my own pastoral experience, I have seen how Scripture can interpret a contemporary situation. Our parish church and halls in Bristol were vast, poorly built, and in imminent danger of falling down. This raised tensions within the Christian community which are familiar from accounts of many similar situations, the tensions involved in having to leave behind the familiar, well-loved structures which God has been seen to bless and use in the past, and to set out into something new and unknown. As might be expected, some were willing to step forward into that unknown, others felt they must hang on to the familiar and make do as best they could with what had always been a blessing to them. I then went on sabbatical and studied Jeremiah from the point of pastoral theology, and saw again his call to the people of Judah to leave behind their familiar city and homeland, and give themselves over to the Babylonians if they were to experience God's blessing in the future. Right there in Jeremiah I found illumination for the situation we faced. The connections at first came to me in what Green would call an 'unclear intuitive hunch', but further study and reflection deepened my conviction that there were many similarities between the two situations, even though they operate on totally different scales, and are of vastly different importance! We shall look at Jeremiah in some depth in Part Three.

This process of interpretation, that starts from an apparently spiritual insight, could easily be subjective in itself; the person or church concerned could simply be choosing biblical passages which suit their own particular purpose and fit their own particular situation. As a result the challenge and questions of the Bible are not heard. It becomes simply a means of confirming what people are already thinking. We are all aware of pastors who constantly preach on their favourite passages of Scripture so as to reinforce a particular message. It is important that the person who believes a scriptural theme or passage is illuminating a situation faced by the church tests that interpretation in a variety of ways. The interpretation must be open to insights and responses from the other members of the Christian community, and, indeed, members of other Christian communities. The church should not concentrate on any one part of Scripture to the exclusion of others. The worship, prayer and preaching of the church should continue to be informed and directed by the range of biblical teaching, as they follow a lectionary or similar means of listening to the whole of Scripture. Christian history will provide examples of other people's use of the same passage or theme, and of how Christians of different ages have responded to similar situations. How can their interpretation, their experience help us today? And every Christian interpreter needs to remember that no human interpretation is infallible; it must always be presented with due humility. The pastor's word is *not* the same as God's word, even though many pastors give the impression that they think it is. The Bible used as interpreter could be used in a purely subjective manner, but such subjectivism can be avoided by a healthy use of the whole Bible.

The biblical image of Christ and his word as *light* seems to encapsulate most clearly this function of the Bible in pastoral theology and work. By bringing the Bible alongside our contemporary experience, that experience can be correctly illuminated and interpreted, and God's work within it discovered.

The Bible in Discipline

One of the goals of Christian pastoral work is surely the creation of a right discipline amongst the members of the Christian community, enabling believers to live a distinctively Christian lifestyle. Unfortunately, as Pattison points out,[21] this function of pastoral care has tended to be ignored in the current century and displaced by an increasing attention to pastoral care as counselling, but in the process much has been lost, not least an understanding in practice of the corporate nature of the Christian life. Even in Christian circles 'the right' is often understood as a matter of personal choice, rather than as having a corporate dimension. Perhaps there has also been a reaction against a type of discipline which was negative, even repressive, and tended to use the Bible as a means of moral blackmail. However, this reaction has undoubtedly gone too far, and we need to reassert the place of discipline in the Christian life, and the role of the Bible in enabling this discipline. One of the features of contemporary church life is an almost total lack of the concept of church discipline, which results in the Church appearing confused and unbelieving.

As Pattison again rightly emphasizes,[22] true Christian discipline is not negative and repressive, but positive and life-giving. It is the outworking of the life of the disciple. The right use of the Bible can enable the development of such discipline, particularly when it is carefully studied within the context of a nurture group, who can use the Scriptures as a means of encouragement of each other, supporting each other in the midst of all that tends to draw them away from a distinctively Christian lifestyle. Pattison warns against the type of discipline which creates a lifestyle so distinctive that it creates barriers for outsiders, a ghetto mentality. Every sect that has arisen on the fringes on the Christian Church has both claimed to be founded on biblical authority, and been marked by tight boundaries. Any one of us who has been confronted by a Jehovah's Witness on our doorstep will be aware of the Witnesses' keenness to justify their beliefs as biblical, and indeed to denigrate many orthodox Christian beliefs as unbiblical. One will also be aware of the narrow mode of thinking into which Witnesses have been encouraged. Open, creative contact and discussion with them seems impossible.

The Bible has often been used in the past to create such a false discipline, but part of a distinctive Christian lifestyle is a commitment to mission, both in terms of evangelism and in social action, proclamation of the work of Christ and service in the name of Christ. However, that mission will only be effective when it proceeds from a community marked by genuine discipleship, discipline that flows from a commitment to Christ.

As we have suggested above in talking about the Bible as Interpreter, the corporate study of Scripture can also help to protect against the wrong use of the Bible as a lever or wand of authority to force people to accept a particular 'discipline'.[23] Christian discipline is largely about the way we live for God in relation to other people, and it is not created when the Bible is left in the hands of just one, or a very few, authority figures; it creates discipline when it is studied and obeyed within the whole Christian community, the Body of Christ. I can so easily interpret the Bible in a way that suits myself; listening to others' understanding of it will correct my self-centred application of its message, and draw me into a richer Christian discipline alongside them.

The Bible in Ethics

One aspect of Christian discipline is ethics. Many pastoral situations will have an ethical dimension, be it on the individual level, one person seeking ethical guidance – 'Should I continue working for this company which manufactures missiles as well as planes?' – or the corporate, a local church deciding how to raise and spend a sum of money, or grappling with what seems to be an example of corporate sin damaging the life of the community or individuals, such as the loss of local green space to a supermarket project. Two points need to be made briefly about the use of the Bible in ethics.

The first is that theology and ethics are inextricably mixed in the Bible. The two cannot be separated. As Oliver O'Donovan, building on Furnish's seminal work on Pauline ethics, points out, Christian ethics must arise from the Gospel of Jesus Christ or it is not

Christian.[24] This must affect our pastoral practice; the person who comes seeking ethical guidance must be helped to see the situation not just in the light of a single ethical choice, but in the light of the whole Gospel. The pastoral situation which seems to exemplify the effects of corporate sin must be subjected to a theological analysis, and not just an ethical analysis. Theology and ethics are one whole in Scripture, and they must be in pastoral work too.

The second point, which follows on from the first, is that biblical ethics cannot be set out from isolated texts; Scripture must be interpreted by Scripture if one is to see the whole field of ethical teaching. The Bible is no more a directory of ethical advice than it is a handbook of pastoral practice. 'We will read the Bible seriously only when we use it to guide our thoughts towards a *comprehensive* moral viewpoint, and not merely to articulate disconnected moral claims. We must look within it not only for moral bricks, but for indications of the order in which the bricks belong together.'[25] There is always a tendency for Christian ethical guidance to be given in the form of proof-texts; this is not only theologically inadequate, but also pastorally dangerous – we can end up dealing with the moral question without also taking account of the Bible's teaching about the nature of the person or people in front of us. A young woman comes in confusion to a minister because she is pregnant and does not know whether it is right to have an abortion. The Bible not only helps us to answer the ethical question about the rightness, or otherwise, of abortion, but reminds us to see this person as God's creation, bearing his image, loved by him, in need of his salvation, a person with a future and a hope. She is not just an ethical quandary to be explored; if she is treated as such, she will probably seek advice elsewhere in the future. A careful use of the whole Bible will enable the ethical issues in pastoral situations to be understood properly in their right context.

The Bible in Worship

Worship is a vital part of Christian pastoral care, because it is about *oikodomia*, the building up of the Body of Christ.[26] Worship focuses the lives of the members of the Christian community on God, and thus deepens people's understanding of their need to trust in God, gives them an identity in their relationship with God, stimulates an awareness of the gifts and needs which they possess, and plays a vital role in preventing personal problems which arise from a lack of trust, a loss of identity, a denial of gifts, a blindness to needs. Pastors naturally encourage those who come to them to discuss a particular need also to come to public worship, not merely out of a desire to increase numbers at their Sunday service, but to enable that person to see their need in the context of God. Apart from that context there will be no genuinely Christian resolution of the situation.

Worship is also inherently corporate, and draws people into the healing community, where they can experience acceptance, first by God in Christ, and, as a result, by their fellow believers. Christian pastoral care is also, I suggest, inherently corporate; all in the Body of Christ have the responsibility of caring for and of building up their fellow members. Modern western society tends to isolate individuals and small family groups, and, as a result, to increase their sense of need. Many people are quite startled by the atmosphere they discover when they first come to join in the Church's worship; they have no previous experience of belonging to a broader community. Worship is the focal and defining point of that community life, as believers are drawn together to focus on God, to remember that they are indeed the people of God. It is also the place where believers are drawn together to focus on each other, and where the different gifts of the Body of Christ are developed for the building up of all. As William Willimon points out, pastoral care is not just about nonjudgemental listening and forgiveness. Worship reminds us of its true, and distinctive, context in Christian truth, the truth of God, and not just in the 'Rogerian myth'.[27]

An essential part of good worship, of course, is the public reading and careful exposition of Scripture, because the Bible is the fount of all our knowledge of God. It therefore plays an essential part in that focusing on God which is so central to worship. Good liturgical practice involves a systematic use of Scripture in the form of a lectionary, or quasi-lectionary, so that the whole message of Scripture can be heard by the believing community, and a liturgical structure which enables scriptural themes to be turned into the elements of worship, praise, confession, intercession, sacramental sharing.

Too much of our worship, however, fails to achieve this. Much protestant worship ignores the lectionary principle, with the result that the choice of Scripture for reading and exposition is left simply in the hands of the minister, resulting frequently in a one-sided view of it. Much strictly liturgical worship within the Catholic tradition fails to link the ministry of the word with the rest of the worship, resulting in a lack of focus. These failures produce not only inadequate worship, but also worship in which the element of pastoral care is obscured. Because people are not clearly built up in Christ through his Word, people are not given a clear sense of their identity in relation to God. More will be said about this in Part Two, when we discuss preaching.

The Bible in Counselling

Much of what has already been said applies to pastoral counselling, because counselling belongs in the broader context of the life of the body of Christ, focused on God by the Scriptures. However, a few additional points about the use of the Bible in this narrow aspect of the broader field of pastoral work need to be made.

First, the counsellor *'should be aware enough to sense the symbolic meaning of the Bible to the parishioner'* (Brabham). To quote the Bible at some individuals may actually have a negative effect, rather than the positive one intended, because of their view of the Bible. Some have perhaps been subjected in the past to an over-authoritative use of the Bible which has been restrictive and guilt-creating, rather than enabling and liberating. The person who most readily enjoys hearing the Scriptures quoted might well be in most need of seeing the broader picture of the biblical revelation. As a young minister I used to spend time talking to an elderly woman who always asked for the same biblical passage, the opening chapter of Ruth, to be read to her; it spoke to her own experience of exile from her adopted homeland as a young mother. Although it was encouraging that someone should ask for the Bible to be read to them at all (I cannot recall anyone else who did!), it became important to introduce her to other texts, so that she could hear the biblical message in a fuller sense. Her Christian life was in danger of remaining stuck at the level of her own experience of nearly sixty years before, whereas she could have been making real progress and enjoying a renewed relationship with God.

Here is certainly a case when the Bible can be used overtly in a counselling situation, to help a person move from one or two texts to a wider view. The skilled counsellor, however, will at the same time show how the Bible can be used to liberate rather than to restrict, and will avoid using the Bible as a stick with which to beat the counsellee. To return to the young woman seeking advice about an abortion, how might the minister talk to her? Which will be more upbuilding to her in her current situation, to say, 'Well, the Bible says so and so, so it's quite clearly wrong,' or to ask, 'Have you ever thought the Bible has anything to say about abortion? What might it be saying that's relevant to your situation at the moment?'

Obviously, where the opposite situation applies, and an individual does not already accept the authority of Scripture in one form or another, a different approach is necessary. If the young woman does not come from a Christian background, she will obviously not know what the Bible has to say on the subject. She is presumably grappling with what her conscience tells her rather than with any biblical texts. In such a case a great deal of preliminary work may need to be done before one can open or refer to the Bible with the person concerned. The ability of the Christian counsellor to discern this symbolic meaning of Scripture can be very important, and significantly affect the way in which a counselling session is conducted.

Secondly, one of the functions of the Bible in counselling is *to enable an individual to turn his or her experiences into prayer.* If the first context of Christian pastoral work is God, then one of the aims of the Christian pastoral counsellor is surely to enable people to pray, to bring their situation to God. And the Bible enables such prayer, both by showing us who God is, that he is a God who delights to hear the prayers of his people and never rejects those prayers, and by giving us examples of prayer, prayers of praise, confession, bewilderment, commitment, anger, frustration. The Christian counsellor who is well versed in the Scriptures will help people to grow in prayer. This does not mean that every pastoral conversation, every meeting with a group, every discussion of a problem, must necessarily be closed by a prayer from the leader; that can be ritualistic. The thoughtful pastor will build prayer out of her own listening to Scripture and the situation, prayer which brings the two together in the presence of God. Sometimes that prayer will be spoken and others encouraged to join with it, sometimes it will be purely inward, a prayer in the pastor's own heart. That pastor, however, will be judging the time when it will be right to share that prayer with the other person or other members of the Christian community.

We need also to consider briefly the vital theological question of whether there is a place for proclamation in counselling, but I shall try to consider that further in the section on 'Truth' in Part Two.

Towards a Pastoral Hermeneutic of Scripture

What then is a pastorally appropriate method of interpreting and using Scripture? The whole question of how we interpret the Bible is at the top of the academic theological agenda at the moment. Christian theologians have been greatly influenced by the growing discipline of 'hermeneutics', how any document is to be interpreted. It is possible to see, in some pastoral writers and thinkers, how these debates have influenced, perhaps at times subconsciously, the way in which they use the Bible. One can certainly find pastoral writers who give very different answers to the question of how the Bible is to be interpreted.

Some, such as Jay Adams – whose thinking I consider in the final part of this book – wish to use a strictly deductive method: one must start with Scripture, a particular passage or a doctrine clearly derived from Scripture, and see the pastoral situation in the light of the biblical revelation. But this constantly fails to prove satisfactory, because it does not recognize what we might call the authority of the situation, or the fact that God is present, at work *in* the situation. Others, such as Laurie Green, demand an inductive method: one must start with the situation, such as the group of Christians forced to wait for their project to come to fruition, or the theological response is bound to be inauthentic. However, as we have already said, and Green himself recognizes, this 'bottom-up theology' is in danger of falling prey to subjectivism. As Cotterell says about libera- tion theology, 'The hermeneutics of liberation theology allow for such a subjectivity in handling the relevant texts as will yield the meanings and significances wished for them.'[28] Unless the 'reflection' element of this process is firmly rooted in some objective under- standing of Scripture, it is difficult to see how the whole process can remain Christian. Michael Williams attempts to discover another hermeneutical method by putting practical theology firmly in the framework of theological ethics,[29] but this seems only an extension of the deductive method, and ties pastoral theology closely to ethics, when it is surely part of the whole theological enterprise.

The 'merging horizons' hermeneutic, associated with Gadamer and Thiselton, perhaps provides the best model for a genuinely pastoral interpretation of Scripture. A 'merging horizons' hermen- eutic insists on reminding the interpreter that the world in which the Bible was written was very different from the world of the modern reader. We cannot immediately assume that we know what the Bible means when it uses a particular word or phrase. The resonance of that phrase today might be very different from its resonance in the time of David or Jesus. We need both to understand the 'horizon' of the biblical world, and that of our own day before we take on the task of bringing the two together.

This hermeneutic has also recently come under criticism from Oliver O'Donovan,[30] on the grounds that it assumes there is nothing in common between our situation and that of the characters and authors of Scripture. But, asserts O'Donovan, there is, because 'past generations occupied the same world as ourselves and can speak with us about it'.[31] All that O'Donovan may be saying is that the task of merging the horizon of Scripture and that of our contemporary experience is not as difficult as it is sometimes stated to be, and that we do not have to be over-careful in selecting aspects of the past horizon, but can genuinely be in touch with the whole perspective of Scripture. Nevertheless, a 'merging horizons' hermeneutic seems to be necessary for pastoral theology if we are to give due weight both to the authoritative Scriptures, written in a particular place at a particular time by particular people, and the reality of the contemporary situation, the particular world which we inhabit. Our hermeneutic must also give a place both to the rest of the Christian tradition with its insights into the correct meaning of Scripture and its centuries of pastoral experience, and to human sciences, which illuminate our contemporary situation, and also have some input into our theology. We are not alone in the task of understanding and applying the Bible. We have the help of two thousand years of Christian teaching and practice, and also the insights granted through those who study God's creation. It may be helpful to express hermeneutic methods in diagrammatic terms. (See opposite.)

If I borrow the word 'response' from Green to replace what I perceive to be Adams' desire for 'solutions', it is because I feel that this is a more genuinely pastoral word. Not every pastoral situation can be neatly solved, but there will be an appropriate pastoral response to make. However, I find Green's 'reflection' a dangerous word; it has no necessary Christian content, although I am sure Green understands it in a Christian way. To keep the Christian focus, I feel we need to give a clear place to the Bible in the whole model.

Adam's method may be depicted as follows:

SCRIPTURE

↓

SITUATION

↓

SOLUTION

Green's method is more complex:

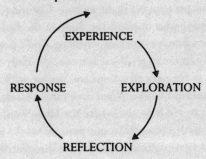

EXPERIENCE

EXPLORATION

REFLECTION

RESPONSE

A merging horizons hermeneutic might look like this:

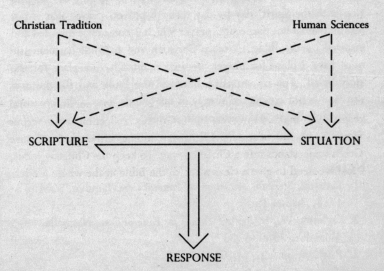

Christian Tradition   Human Sciences

SCRIPTURE   SITUATION

RESPONSE

A True Interpreter

One closing note needs to be sounded, because so far I have failed to make reference to the work of the Holy Spirit. No interpretation of Scripture will be correct unless it is carried out in reliance on the Holy Spirit, the true interpreter of Scripture. The inspirer of Scripture is at work in the Church to enable the Christian community to understand the Scripture. That is why our diagram of the hermeneutic process needs to include Christian tradition, because the Holy Spirit who inspired the Bible in the first place has been at work in the Church ever since, enabling God's people to understand and to apply its message. What is more, the Holy Spirit is at work in the world, in the very situations and people with whom we have to do in our pastoral work. When Scripture is interpreted correctly, it will help us to see how and where the Holy Spirit is at work. When we use the Bible correctly in our pastoral work, when we acknowledge it as a vital pastoral resource, we discover that the Bible itself reminds us that it is the Holy Spirit who gives life to our pastoral theology and our pastoral work. If we may borrow some words from Galatians 5:25 (NIV), also used as a title by J. I. Packer, we 'keep in step with the Spirit' day by day through prayer, prayer that is not just individual but corporate, prayer which is constantly directed and inspired by the Bible. A truly Christian and pastoral hermeneutic must have a place for prayer, because it must have a place for the Holy Spirit. The conversation between the Bible and the pastoral situation is not conducted simply in our minds, but in the presence of the Holy Spirit, and therefore in prayer.

Notes

1. Pattison, Stephen, *A Critique of Pastoral Care*, London, SCM, 1988, chapter 6
2. Oglesby, W., Jr. *Biblical Themes for Pastoral Care*, Nashville, Abingdon, 1980, p. 20
3. Pattison, op. cit., p. 106

4. Peterson, Eugene H., *The Contemplative Pastor*, Grand Rapids, Eerdmans, 1993, p. 77

5. cf. Meiburg, A. L., 'The heritage of the Pastoral Counsellor', in Oates, W., (Ed.), *An Introduction to Pastoral Counselling*, Nashville, Broadman, 1959, pp. 3–18

6. Oglesby, op. cit., *passim*

7. Clinebell, H., *Basic Types of Pastoral Care and Counselling*, London, SCM, 2nd ed. 1984, chapter 3

8. ibid., p. 67

9. ibid., pp. 124–7

10. Deeks, D., *Pastoral Theology: An Inquiry*, London, Epworth, 1987, p. 239

11. Cotterell, P., *Mission and Meaninglessness*, London, SPCK, 1990, p. 248

12. Deeks, op. cit., p. 69

13. Green, Laurie, *Power to the Powerless*, Basingstoke, Marshall, Morgan & Scott, 1987

14. ibid., p. 51

15. ibid., p. 59

16. Green, Laurie, *Let's Do Theology*, London, Mowbray, 1990

17. ibid., chapter 5

18. ibid., p. 78

19. ibid., p. 79

20. ibid., p. 78

21. Pattison, op. cit., p. 63

22. ibid., chapter 4

23. Brabham, D. A., 'Pastoral Counselling and the Interpretation of Scripture', in Oates, op. cit., pp. 222–35

24. O'Donovan, Oliver, *Resurrection and Moral Order*, Leicester, IVP, 1986, chapter 1

25. ibid.

26. Willimon, W. H., *Worship as Pastoral Care*, Nashville, Abingdon, 1979, chapter 1

27. ibid., p. 43

28. Cotterell, P., *Mission and Meaninglessness*, London, SPCK, 1990, p. 257

29. Williams, Michael, in Ballard, P., (Ed.), *The Foundations of Pastoral Studies and Practical Theology*, Cardiff, HOLI 4, 1986, pp. 39–52
30. O'Donovan, Oliver, op. cit., chapter 7
31. ibid., p. 162

Part Two

PROCLAIMING THE
PASTORAL WORD

PREACHING AND PASTORAL CARE

A former colleague of mine grew up in a well-known evangelical parish, a parish particularly known for its preaching ministry. She was a young Christian when the most famous of all its preachers was the incumbent; his sermons were published, and regarded as a model of faithful biblical exposition and clear communication by former generations of evangelicals. However, as he grew older, he began to lose his sight; those were the days before there was any retirement age for clergy, and he continued as the incumbent in spite of being increasingly unable to leave his study and meet people around the parish. Much of the everyday pastoral work with individuals and groups was done by a team of curates, while he concentrated on his preaching ministry, committing many hours of study to sermon preparation. 'What were his sermons like after he became old and his sight deteriorated?' we once asked. 'Well, they were little gems, perfectly formed, but totally detached from real life.'

Preaching and pastoral care belong together. I hope it is obvious that the preacher who only preaches and never meets the people who will listen to the preaching – never gets to grips with the social setting in which they live, never sees them on their own level – will not be able to preach effectively to them, will not be able to teach them. Our God is not a God who has kept his distance and revealed his word to us at one remove; that is not the God of Christianity. Our God is a God who has come into the world, and is active in it, the Creator, Sustainer, Redeemer, the Incarnate One. And it is this

God, this going God, who is the model for Christian mission and pastoral care. One minister I know delights in saying that 'visiting is God's work', because God himself has 'come to visit us in great humility'. Because God has graciously visited us, we must go out to others to reflect his grace. That theological conviction controls the use of this man's time in ministry and the style of the pastoral care he offers; he is constantly visiting people in their homes and, indeed, at their places of work and leisure. God's Holy Spirit is the *parakletos*, the one called alongside to help. That does not mean that we can leave the job of reaching out to him alone, because the Holy Spirit always involves God's people in his work. He is not the one who shouts advice from a distance, but rather the one who comes to live in us and work through us. It is the people of God who are the Temple of the Holy Spirit (1 Corinthians 3:16).

In 1 Thessalonians 2:13 Paul is describing the welcome that the Thessalonians had given to the message he had brought them, and he describes that message as 'the word of God which is at work in you believers'. God's word enters into people's lives; it doesn't stay outside them as some sort of external framework, because it is applied, made real to people by the Holy Spirit who breaks into their lives. It is not just a word of law, but a gracious, pastoral word at work in believers. It is indeed the word of life. The sign that people have really received God's word is not just that their vocabulary changes, but that their lives change. I can still remember one member of a Christian Union group at university bemoaning his failures as a Christian, 'I don't think anything has changed in my life since I became a Christian,' he complained. 'But it has, and it's so clear to us,' came the reply immediately from his two closest friends. They had seen the word of God at work in him.

Scripture in itself is pastoral, it reflects the character of the God who reveals himself in it. Scripture is not systematic – much to the frustration of those who would like to systematize the Christian faith – but rather pastoral. Even where once interpretation tended to reduce Scripture to the level of systematic treatise, more modern scholarship has shown us that that cannot be done without doing violence to the Scripture itself. The classic example of this, of course, is Romans. Romans is *not* Paul writing a systematic theology of justification by grace through faith for the benefit of generations of protestants to come. It is rather a letter that springs out of Paul's own deeply theological reflection on his experience in Christian mission to Jew and Gentile. It springs also out of the experience of the Roman church, there at the heart of the Empire where people from all corners of the world, some Jewish, but most Gentile, some free, some slaves, have together found Christ. It is a pastoral letter, addressing the pastoral needs of a Christian community in a missionary situation — as all Christian communities are!

Paul's other letters are equally pastoral; he responds to the situation of the churches, he doesn't write lectures or tracts for them. Yes, they are profoundly theological, but the theology is worked out against the real background of the recipients and the author, never in a vacuum. The contemporary equivalent of Paul is not the theologian who works in the isolation of study and library, but rather the Christian thinker whose work springs out of direct contact with mission situations. Karl Barth's commentary on Romans made such a profound impact because it grew out of his own experience as a young pastor. In recent years Lesslie Newbigin has been immensely influential in the Church in Britain and North America because his theology, like Paul's, has been forged on the mission field. It is not only Paul's letters that have this stamp of experience; there is a good case to be made for the gospels also being understood best as pastoral, missionary documents. David Bosch's interpretation of Matthew as a missionary work, in *Transforming Mission*,[1] is an outstanding example of such an interpretation.

Old Testament books show an equal refusal to systematize, but rather are set against the background of real situations. Jeremiah's personal, inner struggles, and the struggles of Israel in his day, are the setting in which we learn about the pastoral God. Even the books of the Law come to us in the framework of history; we keep breaking off from law codes to hear something more of the people of Israel's progress and problems. The Writings look for real solutions to people's real needs. Proverbs has often been described as 'sanctified common sense', and both Ecclesiastes and Job can be seen as a struggle for a truer, more pastoral theology over against the type of theology which offers facile responses to complex situations. The Psalms constantly reflect a theology worked out against real human struggles, pains and joys.

A Puritan Example

So if Christian preaching is truly speaking in the name of this triune God, if it is really done in the power of this Holy Spirit, if it is really an exposition of this pastoral Scripture, it will flow out of a commitment to God's work. That work of God is a work of mission in the real world, a pastoral work and not a work simply of study. So I suspect that we must say that the minister who gave up the chaplaincy of the local hospital, which his church had always staffed, on the grounds that his ministry was a 'preaching' ministry and not a 'pastoral' ministry, was at best operating with a false understanding of preaching. If we are truly to preach, and not just to deliver lectures, we must be in touch with the situations, the aspirations, the needs, the joys of the people we shall be speaking to week by week.

Richard Baxter had an immensely influential preaching and pastoral ministry in Kidderminster in the English Midlands in the middle of the seventeenth century. He 'insisted that ministers must preach of eternal matters as men who feel what they say, and are as earnest as matters of life and death require; that they must practise church discipline, to show that they are serious in saying that God will not accept sin; and that they must do "personal work", and deal with individuals one by one, because preaching alone fails to bring things home to ordinary people.'[2] As Baxter himself says, 'I have found by experience, that some ignorant persons, who have been so long unprofitable hearers, have got more knowledge and remorse in half an hour's close discourse, than they did from ten years' public preaching. I know that preaching the Gospel publicly is the most excellent means, because we speak to so many at once. But it is usually far more effectual to preach it privately to a particular sinner.'[3]

Baxter cogently reminds us that the best preaching is pastoral preaching, the preaching of someone who is in regular pastoral contact with the same congregation. Having recently moved from seven years of ministry in a single parish to a situation in which most of my preaching is in different churches, where I have little or no other contact with the people, I know that my preaching now inevitably has less pastoral content. It is therefore, I think, less effective, even if the task of preaching is less demanding for me. Baxter also points us to this necessity of holding together preaching and pastoral care by his own practice. His custom was to spend time with each family in his parish on a regular basis. By visiting seven families for an hour each Monday and Tuesday he could visit virtually all the eight hundred families in Kidderminster every year to catechize them. He recorded later that, of those eight hundred families, seven hundred were converted during the period of his ministry there.

A Puritan born out of time, J. C. Ryle, country clergyman and then Bishop of Liverpool at the end of the nineteenth century, made much the same point as Baxter: 'Do not be above talking to the poor, and visiting your people from house to house. Sit down with your people by the fireside, and exchange thoughts with them on all subjects. Find out how they think and how they express themselves, if you want them to understand your sermons. By so doing you will insensibly learn much. You will be continually picking up modes of thought, and get notions as to what you should say in your pulpit. A humble country clergyman was once asked "whether he studied the fathers". The worthy man replied, that he had little opportunity of studying the *fathers*, as they were generally out in the fields when he called. But he studied the *mothers* more, because he often found them at home, and he could talk to them. Wittingly or unwittingly, the good man hit a nail right on the head. We must talk to our people when we are out of church, if we would understand how to preach to them in the church.'[4]

Our contemporary situation is obviously very different from that of Baxter or Ryle, but they do point up for us today the fact that preaching alone is not a sufficient means of building up the body of Christ; it must be matched by other means of helping people to understand the word for themselves. Most of us will be familiar with house groups and methods of corporate Bible study; it seems to me very important that these run alongside the regular preaching programme of the church. They should be designed with the aim either of complementing the current preaching programme of the church, or indeed of tackling the very same material as is being tackled in Sunday sermons. They give people the opportunity to receive the word in a different setting, and also in a corporate context. Although it might seem that what happens at Sunday worship is corporate because the whole church is gathered, in practice it is a one-dimensional, one-directional experience. The preacher talks to a lot of individuals without any interaction between the members of the body to help them understand and apply the word; but the word of God has not just been given to those with a specific ministry of teaching and leadership. It is God's gift to the whole Christian community, and its meaning will not become fully clear until it is understood within that community. A house group of eight to twelve members also functions as a more natural pastoral unit than the large congregation of several hundreds. It has the ability to focus on individual situations, and to help people to understand their place within the larger context of the whole church. This is not to absolve the clergy of responsibility for a truly pastoral ministry of the word. The minister's task is not just to preach Sunday by Sunday, but to enable others to take their rightful place in the building up of the whole community through a shared ministry. Such a ministry might be even more demanding than one which devolves responsibility for teaching on to one individual alone.

A house group is also pastoral because it offers people another method of learning. For many people the style of the Sunday sermon does not help the learning process; they are not used to taking in information presented to them in lecture or sermon format. Modern communication media never present us with large chunks of uninterrupted words. People are used to receiving information in a whole range of imaginative ways, some of which will communicate to one type of person, some to others. A pastorally minded church will be aware of the manner in which its different members learn best, and offer a variety of styles of teaching to meet that need. The house group will be an appropriate place in which to learn and study the Bible for many people. Equally, the large congregation functions well as a unit of celebration; its pastoral strength is to point people to something far greater than themselves, and to be built up through praise, but effective Christian ministry demands other pastoral strengths that are provided in different kinds and sizes of group.

Worship, preaching and pastoral care

This reminds us, of course, that preaching usually happens in the context of worship. If the aim of preaching is to teach us about the nature of God, then it must lead into worship. The preacher and the listeners must be worshippers or they will not truly be learning what the Bible wants them to learn. Another Puritan, Thomas Adams, complains about an unbalanced view of worship held by some in his day who thought that worship's only function was to provide a framework for preaching:

> Many come to these holy places, and are so transported with a desire of hearing, that they forget the fervency of praying and praising God ... all our preaching is but to beget your praying; to instruct you to praise and worship God ... I complain not that our churches are auditories, but they are not oratories; not that you come to sermons (for God's sake, come faster), but that you neglect public prayer; as if it were only God's part to bless you, not yours to bless God ... Beloved, mistake not. It is not the only exercise of a Christian to hear a sermon; nor is that sabbath well spent that despatcheth no other business for heaven ... God's service is not to be narrowed up in hearing, it hath greater latitude; there must be prayer, praise, adoration ...[5]

Christian preaching is fundamentally linked to Christian worship, and we have already seen that it is fundamentally linked to Christian pastoral care. Therefore we must be constantly thinking about how this three-way relationship is working, how our worship, which includes preaching, functions pastorally. I have written a little about this theme of worship already, but maybe I can make a few more points here.

It may be appropriate to begin with a note of warning, pointed out by William Willimon.[6] One cannot *use* worship to deal with specific and individual pastoral situations, whether it be aiming elements of a service at a particular person, or concentrating in a service purely on a pastoral situation. It is not only that the particular individual targeted invariably fails to turn up to the service or sermon designed for him or her. I can vividly remember congratulating my vicar on one occasion for a particularly good sermon, only for him to complain that it had been written with one person especially in mind, and she had not turned up! More importantly we need to remember that this pastoral targeting is simply not the prime function of worship. Worship, including preaching, is primarily concerned with glorifying God, and it is precisely when worship does truly glorify God that it plays its proper part in pastoral care, because then it focuses people's lives *on* God, and builds them up in him.[7] True worship is worship 'in Spirit and truth' (John 4:24). It is true worship – and therefore true preaching – when the Holy Spirit is at work in it to point men and women to the truth of God, to bring them truly to meet with him. Because this is the Holy Spirit's work, there is an element of unpredictability about the pastoral impact worship will make on people. All of us who preach and lead worship will remember situations when an element of the service, perhaps a phrase in a sermon or a line of a hymn, has had a profound impact on one of those present, even though it seemed quite insignificant to us. Having said that, the reality of the Holy Spirit's work in worship is not an excuse for us to go into worship unprepared. God works through people who walk closely with him, and give him their time in prayer and planning. So the good leader of worship will be aware of the pastoral situation in which the congregation, and not just one or two individuals, meets for worship. That awareness will inform every aspect of preparation for worship, including the preparation for preaching.

The pastorally aware congregation will also come to worship with an awareness of their *neighbours'* joys, sorrows and needs, and be able to focus them on God alongside their own. The community which meets for worship needs to be aware of the wider community of which it is part; the Christian congregation should be both a sign to the world of what God wants communities to be, and also a community which can together minister to the world, pastorally caring for those who are not yet its members. Many churches are very introverted, concentrating on survival, support and social life. This can create a sense of a pastorally caring community, where the members know each other well and look after each other, a place of rich worship and mutual acceptance. But such a community can be very exclusive, its doors shut against the outside world for fear of disturbing the cosiness of its own fellowship. Such a style of fellowship and worship is not, I believe, truly biblical. Preaching could collude with such a denial of mission. But preaching which is pastoral in a biblical sense will inevitably challenge such cosiness. Preaching which takes the Bible seriously must set out great biblical themes: God as the Creator of all, the universal message of the prophets, Jesus Christ as the one who breaks down barriers, the call to universal mission in the power of the Holy Spirit. Such preaching will undermine the falsely 'pastoral' atmosphere of the church and point it towards something more truly biblical.

A pastoral church which is not also a missionary church is, as far as the Bible is concerned, a contradiction in terms. The Bible both demands that Christians be outward looking and outward going in mission, and equips the body of Christ for its mission. Biblical worship therefore, and the biblical preaching which is one aspect of it, should play a part in the pastoral upbuilding not only of those who are present, but also of those who remain outside.

Notes

1. Bosch, David, *Transforming Mission*, Maryknoll NY, Orbis, 1992, chapter 2

2. Packer, J. I., *Among God's Giants*, Eastbourne, Kingsway, 1991, p. 403

3. Baxter, Richard, *The Reformed Pastor*, Wilkinson, J. T., (Ed.), London, SCM, 1956, pp. 186ff.

4. Ryle, J. C., *The Upper Room*, reprinted London, Banner of Truth, 1970, p. 53

5. Adams, Thomas, *Works* 1:103, quoted in Packer, op. cit., p. 336

6. Willimon, W. H., *Worship as Pastoral Care*, Nashville, Abingdon, 1979, p. 49

7. cf. Ward, P., *Worship and Youth Culture*, London, Marshall Pickering, 1993, especially chapter 2

2

PASTORAL PREACHING IN PRACTICE

By definition a discussion of how preaching becomes truly pastoral cannot remain at a purely theoretical level. Every preacher who also desires to be a faithful pastor must consider a range of thoroughly practical questions.

The Practice of Good Pastoral Preaching

Effective pastoral preaching will be aware of a number of factors.

How do these people I am called to preach to learn? As has often been pointed out, most people do not learn by absorbing theory and then neatly applying it to practice. Most people start with what they are currently doing or experiencing, and we should be aware that that is not just true of people in inner-city areas, or of people with a minimum formal education. What I have already said about the use of smaller groups running in parallel to more formal preaching is obviously part of the answer to this question. But it affects also the very style of preaching. The type of illustrations used, the way we structure our sermons, the people we encourage to develop their preaching gifts in the church, the length of our sermons – all this will constantly be under review as we understand more and more about the people of our church through our pastoral contacts with them. Diving straight into heavy biblical expositions just will not work with most congregations – it will sail straight over their heads. That does not mean that our preaching cannot be biblical and expository, but the way we *present* that biblical teaching will vary from place to place according to what we know of the situation in which we preach. When I preach to ordinands in our theological college I can expect to preach for half an hour, I can assume that people will not only have Bibles in front of them but will be able to find their way around them, I can use illustrations from classical music or novels, I can refer to Greek words and constructions, I can use abstract concepts. If I go to take a service for a small congregation in a rural parish which I have never visited before, I can assume none of those things. I need to preach for less time, to sketch in more of the background of a Bible passage, to be ready to say less in a sermon, and to rethink some of my illustrations, perhaps drawing them from the common currency of the week's news. I dare not make assumptions about the way in which people live and worship. I have to preach in a different style, not because there is nobody in that rural parish who could cope with a theological college sermon, there almost certainly is, but because there will be a mixture of people present. They will have different experiences of education, employment and church involvement, and therefore will learn in different ways. As they learn, so I must endeavour to teach.

Good pastoral preaching is gospel preaching. If pastoral concerns affect profoundly the *way* in which we preach, they affect even more profoundly the *content* of our preaching. And at the heart of our pastoral message is the good news of Jesus Christ. That good news is profoundly pastoral, because it tells men and women of the way to forgiveness – the way God has opened up by the offering of his own Son as a perfect sacrifice for sin. It tells men and women of the way to acceptance – acceptance by God, who welcomes us not because of anything we achieve, but solely on the basis of his free gift of his Son. It tells men and women of the way to peace – peace with God, who is able to 'take up our infirmities and carry our sorrows'. The good news of Jesus is profoundly liberating. It enables people to leave the prison of guilt, because it shows them that there is a forgiveness which is not only complete, but also ultimate, forgiveness with God. It enables people to accept themselves, because it shows them that they have been accepted by God quite freely, and it incorporates them into the Body of Christ, the fellowship in which they are accepted by others who reflect to them the gracious welcome of God himself. It fills people with an assurance because it shows that our deepest needs have been provided for, not out of our uncertain achievements, but by the almighty, perfectly reliable God.

But how often our preaching is so much less pastoral than the good news which we claim to proclaim. How easily the preaching of those who make the largest claims to be 'gospel people' slips into Pharisaism, into a setting out of laws, rather than a declaration of wonderful free grace. How easily the ministers of grace present a very different picture to the world:

> *The grim Geneva ministers*
> *With anxious scowl drew near,*
> *As you have seen the ravens flock*
> *Around the dying deer.*
>
> W. E. AYTOUN,
> THE EXECUTION OF MONTROSE

I am very aware that my own preaching is often content simply to place intellectual and moral demands on people. This doubtless results from years of training in highly academic settings, in which reason has been exalted over experience and emotion. The danger is that I present people with something highly polished at the expense of liberating them by opening up the good news for them. This is not to say that there are no demands in the good news. There are, and it is certainly possible to preach the good news in such a way that the grace of God is made not so much free as cheap, as Bonhoeffer put it. There are those who preach such a 'nice' God, that he appears to accept people with no expectation that they need to respond in repentance, belief and obedience. I heard of one minister who said, 'I never preach about repentance. I don't want to be unpopular.' But to present God in that way is not to present the liberating good news. Such a wan, universalist God does not address the deepest needs that we know we have, the need for forgiveness, for acceptance, for peace. There is no justice in this God, because he does nothing about sin, and he does not need to change people. This is not the God of the Bible. And to keep from people the true God is to fail them pastorally; to hide the cost of grace is to hide the glory of the good news. But to say that the good news makes demands is not to say that we can be content with making known the demands on their own; that is to turn good news into bad news.

The story is told of D. L. Moody, the great American evangelist of the last century, who, as a young man, preached a sermon on human sinfulness and the need of human beings to repent and seek forgiveness. The sermon stopped at that point; Moody was planning to follow it up the next Sunday by setting out the good news of all that God has achieved in Christ. That week the Great Chicago Fire broke out, and a number of those who had heard his first sermon were among the victims. Moody vowed that he would never again preach without presenting people with the good news. Good pastoral preaching presents not just the demands, but first the good news of God's salvation in Jesus Christ.

Good pastoral preaching takes account of people's God-given freedom. Too easily the preacher can become the little dictator, ruling his own little world from the platform of his pulpit – 'six feet above contradiction'. Too few of those of us called to the ordained ministry take sufficient account of the power that ministry gives us, and the many subtle, probably subconscious ways in which we can misuse that power. I know of people who have been deeply hurt by such misuse. One preacher over a period of years consistently used his considerable preaching skills to persuade his congregation to take on an increasingly grand building scheme and to give to it. The building now stands as a memorial to him, and a constant reminder to others of feelings of being irresistibly spiritually blackmailed. Another preacher presented a consistently one-sided political subtext to all his sermons. It left some of his hearers feeling that they were not being presented with the living God, but rather the preacher's opinions. A third preached in such a way as to suggest that all was well in his own life, when in fact his family was under immense strain as a result of the criminal behaviour of his son. It needed the intervention of a pastorally-minded church member to enable him to tell his congregation the truth. When he did so, it helped many others to tell him the truth about their own lives, and created an atmosphere of rich, mutual pastoral care between preacher and congregation.

Too much preaching tries to dominate people, rather than leaving them free to consider and meditate on the message, not in a 'take it or leave it' fashion, but in the presence of God. If we dominate people, their response to the message of the good news will not be a free response. But God's free grace demands a free response.

John Stott offers a powerful critique of preaching that seeks to dominate, and points out how that style of preaching fails people pastorally, because it does not lead them to maturity.

> We must never wield the authority of God's Word in such a way as to destroy people's humanness. For God himself, out of love for the people he has made in his own image, addresses us as human beings. He respects the mind and will he has given us; he refuses to coerce us, and instead asks for our thoughtful, loving and free response. Is this not the reason why the biblical writers encourage their readers to develop critical listening? ... This kind of open but questioning mind is implicit even in the 'pastoral' metaphor. Sheep, it is true, are often described as 'docile' creatures, which may be so, but they are fairly discriminating in what they eat, and are certainly not uncritically omnivorous like goats. Moreover, the way in which the shepherd feeds them is significant. In reality he does not feed them at all ... instead he leads them to good grazing pasture where they feed themselves.[1]

We need to keep a careful balance in our preaching between presenting with confidence the good news that everyone needs to hear, and humbly acknowledging our own limitations and other people's freedom – and the lordship of God's Holy Spirit – by refusing to cajole people into a response. Preaching the Word of God is not the same as advertising, which tries to manipulate people into buying a product that they neither need nor want. If we preach

God's Word we must take account of what he has to say about people, and treat them with the respect that they deserve as God's own creation, those who bear his own image. They are not dumb beasts to be herded around, but people with a God-given mind and responsibility. The balance will be difficult to maintain, but good pastoral preaching will not be willing to take short cuts in this area.

Good pastoral preaching will take account of people's feelings as well as their minds. If you have a congregation full of young families, where one spouse is working like stink to pay the mortgage, and the other is constantly exhausted by the demands of small children, then sometimes you just need to pick up their feelings of tiredness, frustration, spiritual inadequacy, and to assure them that it's all right, that God still loves them, they don't have to have nice, regular evangelical quiet times for God to maintain his interest in them, that they can rest in and rely on the God who 'gives power to the faint and strengthens the powerless' (Isaiah 40:29). I once preached a sermon that did not say much more than that to our congregation in Bristol, and it really struck a chord. It involved my operating against my usual rather dry, intellectual style of preaching, but the effort was well worth it. In a largely elderly congregation, or one with a strong representation of students, other emotions will be present; the good preacher will always be aware of those emotions, and sometimes need to pick them up quite overtly.

Preaching at occasional offices also often involves our picking up people's feelings and acknowledging them. It would be easy to assume that the dominant emotion at a funeral is that of sadness, the mixture of aloneness and numbness that accompanies a bereavement. But there are often other emotions present, and some of those may be nearer the surface at the service itself. There is often a great deal of guilt, anger and confusion around at funerals, and we fail pastorally if we do not pick this up, gently and skilfully.

Most funerals are not overtly traumatic; but all preachers will have officiated at some that are. I can recall having to take three such funerals within a matter of a few months, when I was an incumbent. Readers may find it helpful to evaluate the sermons I preached at these funerals. One was for a soldier in his twenties who had taken his own life while on a tour of duty in Northern Ireland, apparently following a difficult phone call.

1 Corinthians 15

N will be missed a great deal. That, of course, hardly needs to be said, especially to you, his family and friends, who will remember so much love given and received throughout his life, and you who represent his second family, the Army, who have enjoyed his companionship and loyalty, and given him such friendship and so many opportunities in return, a second family who have shown what you thought of N and how much you miss him by the care you have shown to his first family over the last few days. And maybe that sense of missing N is heightened by the manner of his death, the tragedy of it, when all those who have been close to him naturally ask all sorts of questions of themselves. We know, I'm sure, that nobody can in any way be blamed for N's death, but it's not always so easy to control our thoughts and feelings when we are missing someone so much, and maybe some of those thoughts and feelings are making us miss him all the more.

It is possible to miss someone in a very negative way, to think only of the fact that someone is 'gone', but to be negative like that is not, of course, the Christian way. Our watchword is borrowed from those words of St Paul we just read in 1 Corinthians 15 – 'Thanks be to God.' – Our hearts and minds should always be full of thanks to God for *all* that he gives us, and we learn also to give thanks for those who have died. If we are tempted to say, 'Oh, I do miss so-and-so' when someone we love greatly has died, we must learn rather to say 'Oh, I do thank God for him.' Because a life is a gift from God, we can thank him for that gift, and so we never have to be negative when we miss someone. Some words that mean a great deal to N's parents and their family at the moment sum that up so well – 'Say not in grief that he is no more, but in thankfulness that he was.' Say thank you to God for N, for what he meant to you, for his love of nature and the world around him, for his directness, which made him call a spade a spade and pâté meat paste, for the times you spent with him, and all the good things you received from him. And maybe in our thankfulness we can remember to be thankful for the men and women of our security forces who on our behalf show such commitment and soak up so much pressure, especially in Northern Ireland.

And, as we thank God for N, we must learn to thank God as Paul does there in 1 Corinthians 15 – 'Thanks be to God, who gives us the victory through our Lord Jesus Christ.' We are not just thankful to God for his gift of a life which has touched ours; we are most thankful because our Lord Jesus Christ has won a victory over death. Because he himself died, and then rose again from death, he has conquered the power of death. Not only has God given us life, for which we thank him, he has given us also everlasting life in Christ, for which our thanks is even greater.

So N will be greatly missed, but never, I hope, in a negative way, because, as you miss him, you will give thanks to God for him. And we shall remember with even greater thanksgiving this great truth, that, in Jesus Christ, there is a victory, a victory which can transform all our negative thoughts, and all our fear and anxiety in the presence of death, because it is a victory over death itself.

The second was for a much-loved member of our church, who died after she was knocked over by a car travelling at no more than a few miles per hour. Her husband was also slightly hurt, and the accident happened as they left a church lunch. They were just beginning to enjoy the freedom of retirement, and had numerous community involvements as well as several young grandchildren to dote on.

Romans 8:31–39
Most of us are here today feeling a deep sense of shock, because we have been so suddenly and painfully separated from N, whom we have loved so much. The pain of separation has been heightened because we had no time to say 'Goodbye', no time to

say 'Thank you', no time to say 'I love you'. But, of course, to pick up some words we've just heard in Romans 8, we have not been separated from N's love. She has left us such a rich inheritance, an inheritance of love, firstly as a wife and mother and mother-in-law and grandmother, an inheritance which will carry on growing, accruing as you carry on growing together as a family, never forgetting N, always thankful for the love which she has left you and which will forever enrich your family life. And all of us who have received so much as N's friends know that we shall always benefit from the love she has shown us, always that welcoming smile, that ability to listen and understand, that readiness to visit so many people in their homes, that hospitality which invited so many into her home, that constant encouragement, that gentle refusal to let people, and most of all clergymen, take themselves too seriously, all of that love springing from a deep and growing faith in God who loved N and whom N loved.

We are not separated from N's love, but let's remember those original words of St Paul – verse 35. However good we are, however Christian, we are not exempted from the tribulations and pains of life in this world, as N's death reminds us. But, whatever happens to us, however painful, we are not separated from God's love, the love he has shown us in Jesus Christ who, as Paul says, died, was raised from the dead, is at the right hand of God his Father, and is interceding, praying for us. Nothing can separate us from his love. Death can't. N's life on this earth may have ended, but her eternal life has begun; she is with God, with the Lord Jesus Christ, experiencing, rejoicing in the glory of his love with all the barriers, all the limitations of life in this world, swept away. Death doesn't cut us off from the love of God, it actually opens the door into that love so wonderfully that our minds can hardly even begin to imagine it.

And death doesn't cut *us* off from the love of God, us who remain living through the tribulations and pains of this earth. We feel the pain of separation from N, but God's love is just as real and as present as ever, and I think we have seen that in the outpouring of love from so many people which has so touched and strengthened N's family over the last week. And you will continue to be strengthened by N's legacy of love to you, by the faith which you share with N, faith in the God who loves us and will never let us go, and the assurance that, whatever pain we go through, even death, we are only stepping further on into the love of God, the love which N now knows perfectly, and which we shall one day also know and share with her.

We have come here today bearing the pain and shock of separation. But I believe that N would want us to go away with something more than just that pain; I believe that she would want us to take away a fresh glimpse of the love of God and a fresh assurance that nothing can separate us from that love — verses 38–39.

The final funeral was that of a sixteen-year-old who was killed, along with a friend, whilst joy-riding in a stolen car. His family had experienced a whole series of bereavements in recent years. A girlfriend had also been in the car; her life had been saved by a seatbelt.

Luke 23:32–43

We want to give thanks today for the life of N; in doing that we're not going to ignore the terrible, and indeed, unnecessary manner of his death, but first we need to be thankful for his life. That life was too brief, but in it he gave a great deal. He gave to his family [... *add family information provided by them*]. Those family memories will stretch right back across his life; some of N's friends will also be able to look back across his whole life, others will have only known him more recently, as a typical sixteen-year-old, with his loud music and his enjoyment of motor mechanics and his love of animals. And all of us, family and friends, those who've known him for years, those who've only just become his friends, we can all take our memories of N and turn them into thanksgiving today. We thank God for this typical sixteen-year-old, who just felt, as we all do when we're sixteen, that he had to be what others wanted him to be – and that perhaps was why death came to him so suddenly, so tragically.

And it was an awful, tragic death, and this week I've seen the pain which it has brought to this family, and let's remember that there's another family bearing their pain to another funeral on the other side of our city right now. Please listen now if you find it a thrill to take cars, and never, never, never do it again, because I don't ever again want to have to stand in front of a family in the pain that this family is in today. And I'm not just a vicar, I'm also a parent, and I don't want to find myself in a few years' time sitting where N's family are today. As we remember N, can we please also learn a lesson from him and his death today?

N's death will naturally make us remember his life, it should make us feel real thankfulness for his life, and I hope it will teach us something too. But it also provokes all sorts of other feelings, other questions that we need to bring out into the open today. Why did this tragedy happen? Why does God allow this suffering if he's really in charge? Why? And, of course, there's no neat answer to that question, but there is a very important truth to remember in those verses from the Bible we've just read, verses which tell us about Jesus, God's own Son, and his death on the cross. God's own Son suffered dreadfully and died. God is not a far-off, distant, unfeeling God; he knows about pain and suffering, he knows what it means to watch his own Son die. He's not sitting out there somewhere quite unable to understand how we feel today, he's here with us, sharing our pain because he knows what it means to suffer for himself.

All of us have asked that question 'Why?' over the last week, and I suspect we've all asked another question: 'If only ...?' There's no one here today who doesn't feel in some way guilty about N's death; 'If only I'd done so and so.' And we could spend the rest of our lives being chewed up, destroyed by that guilt. But listen to what Jesus said as evil men nailed him in agony to his cross – verse 34. Jesus prayed for the forgiveness of his own murderers, because Jesus *always* offers his forgiveness; in the end we can only deal with our guilt when we know that God has dealt with it, and he did when he sent Jesus to die for us. Jesus who was perfect took on himself all that is wrong in us so that we could know his forgiveness. And Jesus has a message, a prayer for everyone here today – 'Father, forgive them.' God doesn't want you to be eaten up by guilt, but rather to discover the wonder of his forgiveness.

I think there may also be some people here today, and especially those of you who were N's friends, the same age as his, who feel as though there isn't much hope left for you now. To have a friend die in these circumstances is shattering, and when at the same time you have to live in a world where there aren't many jobs, and people don't seem very interested in the prospects for teenagers, then you can give up hope. But listen to the conversation Jesus had with one of the criminals executed with him – verses 42–43. Nobody was ever in a more hopeless position than that criminal, because he was actually hanging on a cross, waiting to die. And right there Jesus gave him hope, a promise of hope. There is hope if we are prepared to look for it in Jesus; life isn't meaningless if we're prepared to let God into our lives. And if one person takes away from this service today the message that there is hope, and as a result refuses to take a car, refuses to take that risk of death, and begins to look forward to building a new life, then in a small way good will have come out of N's death, hope will have come out of it. This could seem like a hope-less day, but I believe that in fact God wants us all to take away with us a message of new hope.

The emotions present at those funerals were very complex. It would have been quite inadequate to offer a standard funeral, and preach a standard funeral sermon on these occasions. Each one demanded a considerable amount of time in preparation, together with the family, with especial thought being given to the selection of Scripture passages and the writing of sermons. Those sermons had both to express the biblical hope of life triumphing over death, resurrection overcoming tragedy, and to acknowledge the complex tangle of emotions people were feeling. People needed to know not only that those emotions were quite natural, it was not wrong to feel them, but also that the Lord who bears our sorrows was capable of bearing their anger, guilt and confusion as well as their sadness.

It may seem obvious to acknowledge the emotional nature of a funeral, but marriages and baptisms are also powerfully emotional occasions. The emotions around at a wedding can be almost explosive, and at the very least people will be very nervous. If preachers at weddings can pick that anxiety up and affirm it – 'It's OK to shake a bit – after all, you don't do this very often' – then perhaps we are beginning to communicate, and can go on to take account of some of the other emotions around. These may relate to the presence of people whose own marriages have failed, or who are living with partners outside of marriage, or the feeling of parents that have been abandoned. This is not an occasion for voicing such emotions openly in a sermon, but of being aware of them, and subtly acknowledging them.

At an infant baptism the family's most prominent emotion is probably a real desire to say 'Thank you' for the baby. The preacher who dives straight into covenant theology has probably lost them straight away, because the sermon is not on the family's wavelength at all. Of course, there might be other emotions present, especially if the child is seen as 'illegitimate', or there are single family members present, or you have a number of people in your church facing the problem of infertility. How might these affect the style and content of the sermon on such an occasion? The preacher who asks that question has begun to prepare a pastorally appropriate sermon for such an occasion.

An adult baptism can also be an emotional event, especially if the baptism marks a decisive commitment of an individual stepping outside the traditional patterns of their family. Good pastoral preaching will acknowledge and affirm those feelings, and show how God's word relates to them, because God accepts the people who have them. The baptism itself is a sign of that acceptance; its own pastoral nature demands pastoral preaching to complement it.

Good pastoral preaching will also be prepared to take people's actual situation seriously, and be prepared to look at it closely and analyse it.

If someone comes to you for counselling, they will not continue to come if they think you are not taking them seriously; in the same way, if someone comes to your church, they probably will not keep coming if they think that your preaching does not take them seriously. If they do keep coming, it may be for the wrong reason, that they do not want their own situation to be addressed and changed. The sermon is part of the 'escape' from the real situation that a church unfortunately sometimes provides. The situation in which preaching constantly avoids actual situations is one in which people are very unlikely to grow personally and spiritually.

Donald Capps offers a profound, but helpful, analysis of the links between preaching and pastoral care. He shows how both good preaching and good pastoral counselling share a similar structure, with four stages common to both: identification of the problem, reconstruction of the problem, diagnostic interpretation, and, finally, pastoral intervention.[2] Diagnostic interpretation, he goes on to say, does not require special expertise, but is simply the application of the Gospel to the situation.[3] He then sets out six types of theological diagnosis used both in sermons and in pastoral counselling.[4]

Let us briefly look at one of these types of theological diagnosis, the first in Capps' list. This is theological diagnosis which identifies the underlying personal motivations which cause the problem, in other words, digging deep into people's feelings and attitudes to unearth the source of the situation. This is both a standard tool of the preacher, and also a standard tool of the counsellor. In marital counselling, for instance, the counsellor will often need to help the counsellee realize for herself or himself the unhelpful attitude which has brought the marriage to its current point. In a sermon on marriage, the preacher will attempt to draw out, this time in general terms but based on experience of particular situations, the motives that can lie behind marriage breakdown in society as a whole. As Capps points out, this is theological when the congregation, or the individual counsellee, is enabled to see their motives in the light of God's will, and enabled to move on to repentance, thanksgiving and change as appropriate. I think there is quite a lot for any preacher to meditate on there. Good pastoral preaching is serious business, it involves serious analysis and investigation of people's situations, and a serious attempt to see those in the light of God's will for them.

The Practice of Bad Pastoral Preaching

If preaching can play a powerfully effective part in the wider pastoral ministry of a church, so, as we have already seen, it can have a disastrous effect pastorally. Let me try to set out a few examples of pastorally bad preaching.

Preaching is bad when preachers assume that they know the feelings or situation of people when they don't. There is a general pastoral point here. One colleague of mine vividly remembers an encounter from the early days after his ordination. His parish was responsible for a hospital chaplaincy, and he was visiting people on a gynaecological ward. One woman was trying to explain to him how she felt after her recent hysterectomy. 'I know just how you feel,' said the green young curate in an attempt at sympathy. 'Oh no, you ****** well don't!' came the reply. He learnt an important lesson in that brief conversation.

But that lesson can apply to preaching as well. One of the occasional duties for clergy in one city where I worked was to go and speak at assembly in the Church of England comprehensive school. One of my colleagues caused major problems in this school when he spoke just after a sixth-form field trip to the south coast. 'We all know the sort of thing that goes on on a school field trip,' he said, 'it's a great opportunity to hunt out a new girlfriend or boyfriend, as well as get in a few from the off-licence.' Now he thought he was really getting on the wavelength of his hearers, but in fact the sixth-formers were deeply offended by what he said; it just was not true. These were all young people from local churches, they had moral standards and, what is more, they took their work seriously; they had gone on the field trip to study and not to indulge themselves. They made their feelings clear to the headmaster, and those feelings were made very clear to the rest of us who went into the school. If we do not really know a situation well, and even when we think we do, we should never assume that we understand people's feelings and attitudes – it can be pastorally disastrous.

Preaching can also be pastorally unhelpful, or even disastrous, because of the danger of generalization. Preaching by definition tends to cover large canvasses with a broad brush, but we need to be aware that broad brush strokes can create quite a lot of mess. It is very easy to drop into a sermon some ill-thought out phrase – 'homosexual perverts ... the Jews killed Jesus ... divorce is always sinful ... German Nazis' – but perhaps your congregation contains people who know the pain of having a homosexual orientation but who in fact live lives that are a lot holier than yours, perhaps that particular Sunday someone will have brought along a Jewish friend, who certainly was *not* responsible for killing Jesus, perhaps a divorced member of your congregation was abandoned by her husband and has lived for years with her own guilt because she eventually agreed to a divorce, perhaps one of your congregation had a German grandparent who spent years opposing the Nazi government, and perhaps those people will not bother to come again and listen to you preach.

I do not want to imply that we can never speak directly when we preach, but we do need to think about whether what we are saying, and the way we are saying it, is genuinely Christian. Is what I say and the way I say it genuinely going to build up the people in front of me? We also need to remember that, even after several years of ministering in one place, we will not always know the precise situation of people in front of us. In a city church there will nearly always be someone present whom we do not know, and even when we do know them it may take some people a lifetime to reveal their innermost pastoral needs to a pastor. It may take years to discover the hidden forces that make a congregation behave in the way it does. I remember that it took me over a year to discover just who was related to whom in one parish where I worked! The complex of family ties within the congregation was an important element in the whole manner in which the church operated.

Drawing close to people pastorally, getting involved in a community pastorally, is risky, because it exposes us and our limitations. The preacher who sits in his or her study all week probably makes few mistakes because the preaching that results takes few risks, but does such a preaching ministry really build up the people of God where they are? Such preaching may feel safer, easier, because it does not have to grapple with the real situation, it does not take the risks involved in allowing Scripture and situation to have a real conversation with each other. But Scripture will say penetrating things to real situations; real situations will demand a depth in our understanding the Scriptures and will challenge sloppy exegesis of them. I am convinced that one of the features of a good preacher is a pastoral heart, which refuses to take refuge in safety, but is always ready to engage with pastoral and scriptural truth.

Notes

1. Stott, John, *I Believe in Preaching*, London, Hodder & Stoughton, 1982, pp. 176f.
2. Capps, Donald, *Pastoral Counselling and Preaching: A Quest for an Integrated Ministry*, Philadelphia, Westminster, 1980, chapter 2
3. ibid., chapter 3
4. ibid., chapter 4

COUNSELLING AND
PROCLAMATION

It should be clear to those readers who have arrived at this point that I do not believe that Christian pastoral work can be equated with counselling. The Bible's vision of the pastoral task is much broader than care for individuals in problem situations, although such care is certainly not excluded by the Bible. However, we have to recognize that much of the literature on Christian pastoral work does centre on issues related to counselling. In North America, in particular, pastoral care has in this century been largely reduced to counselling. Evangelicals, Liberals and Catholics have all tended to concentrate on counselling in their pastoral writing.

In our own consideration of the relationship of preaching to pastoral care, we therefore need to consider a little more fully the narrower but still vital theological question of whether there is a place for proclamation in counselling. What is the relationship of preaching, which is essentially corporate, to counselling, which deals essentially with individuals? Is the purpose of counselling to communicate revealed Christian truth? Those wedded to an entirely non-directive, strictly Rogerian approach to counselling would doubtless give a negative answer to this question. For them the counsellor's role is simply to listen, to be open to the counsellee, to allow people to tell their story in their own terms. Careful listening shows that we are 'with' people, and helps to heal by its open acceptance. One can see how this approach could become quite inimical to any sense that proclamation has a place in counselling. Others, however, have been far more positive in their approach.

Proclamation as Listening

Eduard Thurneysen was a Swiss Reformed pastor whose own ministry was closely associated with that of Karl Barth, perhaps the most influential theologian of the twentieth century. As one might expect from that tradition, Thurneysen gives a high place to proclamation in his understanding of pastoral ministry, and accepts the relationship between counselling and proclamation in positive terms. Thurneysen sees proclamation happening in pastoral conversation because such conversation is a matter of *listening*, not just by the counsellor to an individual, but by both parties to the Word of God.[1] However, as Jacobs points out, Thurneysen does not really consider *how* one brings these two together. Listening is, of course, a vital element in a pastoral conversation, but how does the listening of one party to the other become a mutual listening to the Word of God? A number of other things need to be in place before one can assume that such a conversation becomes a mutual listening to God's Word, not least a theological assumption that God speaks, and the spiritual maturity involved in knowing how to listen to him and discern his voice above the many others that crowd into our brains. Without wanting to say that the question of how proclamation happens is a simple one to answer, one's reaction to Thurneysen is that his approach is too vague to be really helpful. He is right to acknowledge that in any Christian ministry there must be an element of 'waiting upon the Lord', an openness to the unexpected, but he seems to be adopting an approach so passive that it ignores the equally biblical demand that the good news of Jesus Christ needs to be actively made known.

The Christian Counsellor and the Christian Community

A far more robustly positive answer to the question of whether there is a place for proclamation in the counselling session is given by Jay Adams. Adams sees proclamation and counselling as holding together in the *person* of the counsellor, because he believes that one can be a counsellor only if one is also a preacher.

> Counselling, like preaching, is a ministry of the Word ...: it is, therefore, an integral part of the pastor's ministry. He is a pastor-teacher (Ephesians 4:11), not merely a teacher only. Pastoral work involves ministry of the Word to individual Christians ... Public and private ministry of the Word are of a piece and supplement (and contribute to) one another. When a pastor (who has been counselling) preaches, he does so differently from the one who preaches only. When a preacher counsels only, he does so differently than if he also preaches. The former is more down-to-earth in his preaching; it sounds less bookish. People begin to say, 'He knows! He understands my problem,' and they come for counsel. A preacher who preaches as well as counsels, on the other hand, counsels more biblically – because in order to preach, he must continually expound the Scriptures. From this exposition, greater confidence develops, and he has more help to offer his counsellees. The two go together. In fact, whenever one is separated from the other, both suffer.[2]

Adams' approach is helpful here, and reflects something of the richness of the Puritan pastoral tradition seen at its best in Richard Baxter's ministry. As we have already noted, it is vital that the preacher is in one-to-one contact with those to whom he or she will preach. Whether one wants to call that individual contact by the rather technical name of 'counselling' is irrelevant. Pastors were building those contacts with people for centuries before the terminology of 'counselling' was invented in the twentieth century. The best pastors have always recognized that pastoral contact is a key element in good preaching.

However, I wonder whether Adams may be going too far in his parallel insistence that the counsellor must also preach. Is that really the calling of every person to whom God has given gifts that can be well used in the pastoral care of individuals, families and groups? In practice that would not seem to be the case, and the biblical picture of ministry would seem to suggest that there are ministries that involve preaching and proclamation, and others that are concentrated more on caring (cf. Paul's list of gifts for ministry in 1 Corinthians 12:28 and the different types of ministry set out in 1 Timothy). Many are called to pastoral roles which do not have a specific element of teaching or preaching enshrined in them. That does not mean, however, that their ministry is unbiblical, or contains no element of proclamation.

An article by J. L. Elder may profitably be set alongside Adams' ideas to produce a slightly more rounded picture. Elder emphasizes the fact that pastoral counselling belongs in the context of the Christian community, where proclamation and teaching also take place; counselling is not an isolated activity separated from the rest of the life of the worshipping, learning community.[3] Counselling is never a purely individualistic matter. This links us back to what we have already noticed about the breadth of a truly biblical picture of pastoral care and also about the function of worship as pastoral care. Counselling is not the whole of Christian pastoral care, it stands beside preaching, teaching, worship, fellowship, mission, the whole life of the Body of Christ, the essential corporateness of the Christian life.

However, Elder fails to deal with the situation of someone coming from outside the Christian community to seek counselling with a Christian counsellor or pastor. Adams' answer to this situation would probably be to tell the person to start attending church, so that they can clearly hear the Gospel and respond to it: until there has been such a response, there can be no real progress in the counselling encounter. In Part 4 I spell out my reservations about Adams' approach at this point.

Both Elder and Adams also fail to recognize a situation which may be more common in the United Kingdom and some other countries than in their home country of the USA. This is the situation in which a Christian is employed to work as a counsellor in a secular environment, such as the National Health Service or the state sector of education. In such a setting any overt evangelism or proclamation by the Christian counsellor is out of the question; there is no possibility of the Christian taking the initiative to impose a spiritual solution on the counsellee. Some of those committed to a very clear 'Christian counselling' position might say that it is impossible for a Christian to work as a counsellor in such a setting. Others would want to be more positive, and be keen that Christians should not avoid being involved in a secular context. The environment of the whole counselling service will be enriched by the presence of mature Christians. There will be people involved who will not dismiss religious feelings and ideas as irrelevant, or evidence of immaturity, or even dangerous. Such an attitude to religion has often held sway in the world of psychology, particularly in that area of it strongly influenced by Freud. If Christians fail to play their part in such secular settings they cannot then complain if anti-religious views are allowed to reign unchallenged in psychiatric or other counselling services provided by the state.

But let us return to Adams and Elder and the possibility of making some connection between their positions. Adams is right, I suggest, in making a personal link between proclamation and counselling. The connection between the two does lie in the person who does the counselling. But Elder is also right to stress the importance of the community. No one is a solitary Christian, not even the highly qualified counsellor. That counsellor may also be a preacher, in which case the person who comes for counselling probably assumes that there will be an element of proclamation in the counselling session, although one hopes this can be offered subtly. In that setting a counsellee will expect there to be a mutual exploration of a passage of Scripture, or a discussion of biblical themes or stories that relate to the situation. It will seem natural to turn the discussion into prayer. The counsellee may want and need a clear explanation of biblical moral standards. It will not seem odd to the counsellee if the preacher-counsellor suggests that he seek out Christian worship and fellowship, or follows up some of the biblical ideas for himself.

But that counsellor may not be a preacher. This counsellor may even be operating in a situation where the counsellee has not chosen to speak to any particular person, but has been allocated a counsellor through a purely impersonal process. Religious commitments may have played no part in the process of seeking counselling. Such a counsellor, however, is no less a member of the Christian community than the preacher. The Christian counsellor, in whatever situation she is working, needs the support of the Christian community, its worship and its ministry of the Word. The counsellor may not be called to be a preacher as well, but she is called, like any other believer, to be mature in Christ, and that involves being constantly built up through the Scriptures. Without such support a counsellor will not be kept focused on Christ, she will not be growing in holiness. When a person is growing in holiness, however, it will communicate to the people with whom she comes into contact. There will be times when the counsellee will ask questions that are prompted by the counsellor's own character; it is normally quite appropriate for the counsellor to declare her own Christian commitment in response to such a question, even when it is asked in a purely secular setting. When the counsellor becomes aware that there is a religious element to the counsellee's situation, it will not be inappropriate to try to open that up by gentle questioning. The counsellee will indeed have been failed if that key element has been ignored or not taken seriously.

The proclamation may happen in different ways in different settings; we cannot say that proclamation will or must always happen in a particular way. Sometimes it will be more verbal than others, sometimes it will have clear, immediate results. But in the different situations there is still proclamation, and in each case the link between proclamation and counselling is personal; it is located not so much in a method as in the person of the counsellor. However, although it is personal, it is not individualistic. In every case the Christian community plays its part, because no Christian counsels in isolation from that community, the Body of Christ, of which every Christian is by definition a member.

Biblical Models for Proclamation

Donald Capps offers a much more thorough investigation of the links between counselling and proclamation, trying to understand those links in terms of different types of biblical literature. He suggests that in counselling proclamation happens, not always in a directly verbal fashion, but through the *relationship* of counsellor and counsellee.[4] The person of the counsellor is therefore very important for Capps, but he moves us on to look at the more subtle question of how the counsellor relates to the person who comes seeking help. He offers three biblical models for this process. The first he calls the non-directive or 'Psalmic' model, which one might associate with Rogers, in which the Psalms become an example of the open sharing of feelings, be it anger, bewilderment, joy or shame.

Secondly there is the directive or 'Proverbic' model, used by Adams, in which the Proverbs, with their pithy offerings of 'sanctified common sense', are taken as a biblical justification for the giving of advice in a direct form in counselling. Finally there is the indirective or 'Parabolic' model, in which Jesus' parables, or Old Testament stories such as Nathan's parable to David (2 Samuel 12), are taken as an example of how people can be helped to understand their situation, and what God is saying to them in their situation, through indirect means, including the use of story.

Capps criticizes the non-directive model as failing to include the Christian element of transformation, and the directive model as failing to take seriously the feelings of the counsellee. The indirective model, he feels, both starts where we are, and then changes our perceptions. A parable, by restructuring our perception, is proclamation. David is moved to confession and repentance only when the reality of his sin is brought home to him by Nathan's parable (2 Samuel 12:5–7, 13). He hears God's Word to him, and is transformed, through a story.

Capps makes some valid points here, but perhaps falls into the trap of many writers on pastoral counselling, who want to commit themselves to one, single method as the best, or even the most scriptural. The Bible contains Psalms, Proverbs and parables, and, in fact, many other kinds of literature. If we take seriously the different types of literature in the Bible as an aspect of God's revelation of himself, as models of the way in which God speaks, we need to acknowledge that proclamation can happen non-directively, directively and indirectively. Proclamation may happen through listening; it may happen in the person who, as a member of the Christian community, cannot help but hold together the twin Christian concerns to proclaim the Word of God and to care for those in need; it may happen through a caring and creative relationship; it may happen through an imaginative use of story or parable to help people change their perceptions of their own situation, and, most importantly, their perception of God.

Maybe a genuinely scriptural approach will not be content to use just one scriptural model let alone one secular model, but will discover a range of manners in which one can hold together proclamation *and* counselling. We are not in a position to choose one or the other of these emphases. We cannot jettison either proclamation or pastoral care, because both are part of our Christian calling set out in the Bible. We are called to hold together the truth and care which are both vital ingredients of the process of Christian upbuilding, the pastoral task, in Paul's words, of presenting whole people 'mature in Christ' (Colossians 1:28).

This must have major implications both for the individual called to any kind of pastoral ministry, and to the Church, with its calling to be a pastoral community. None of us can be content with going down one road of pastoral care, with adopting one style of counselling, or indeed with endorsing just one style of preaching. The Bible itself points us to a rich variety of approaches, because it contains a rich variety of types of literature, through all of which God speaks. Human needs are equally varied. And the gifts and talents God has given to the Church are diverse. Not everyone is called to be a preacher, but everyone is called to submit to God's truth as he has revealed it in the Bible, and to witness to that truth as a member of the Body of Christ. For most people that witness will not be the proclamation of an evangelist, but the offering of their own gifts to the proclamation of the whole Church. Not everyone is called to be a counsellor, but every member of the Body of Christ is called to reflect to the rest of the Body, and to those outside the Body, that love and care which Christ has shown us. For most people that will not involve becoming trained, professional counsellors, any more than it will mean their becoming preachers. It will mean rather their contributing their own gifts to the whole Church's task of caring, learning and teaching. We need to be sure that, under the direction of Scripture, we are using those diverse gifts to respond to the needs of the people God is bringing to us.

Notes

1. Thurneysen, Eduard, in Jacobs, M., (Ed.), *Faith or Fear?*, London, Darton, Longman & Todd, 1987, pp. 84–7
2. Adams, Jay, *A Theology of Christian Counselling*, pp. 279f.
3. Elder, J. L., in Oates, W., (Ed.), *An Introduction to Pastoral Counselling*, Nashville, Broadman, 1959, pp. 203–10
4. Capps, Donald, *Pastoral Counselling and Preaching: A Quest for an Integrated Ministry*, Philadelphia, Westminster, 1980, chapter 5

4

TRUTH IS PASTORAL

'What is truth?' asks Pilate in John 18:38. There was a generation of biblical scholars who interpreted his question as one of mystification concerning Greek and Hebrew conceptions of truth. 'What is truth? Is it what the Greeks think it is, the abstract concept of what corresponds with reality, a reality that is often unseen, as in Platonic thought, in comparison with the falsehood of much of what is visible? Or is truth what the Hebrews think it is, something much more personal, less abstract, fundamentally a quality of God, his own truthfulness and therefore his trustworthiness, all of which should be reflected in his people?'

There are two problems with this now somewhat old-fashioned interpretation of Pilate's question. It could only be held by people who have not read the Old Testament, where the Hebrew word *'emet* can quite clearly mean what corresponds with reality just as much as it refers to a characteristic of God, and, of course, it could only be held by people who have not read John's gospel up to that point. We who have read that gospel know that Pilate is not grappling with a nice point of philosophy. He is *looking* at the truth, the man standing in front of him. 'Behold the man,' was the only way Pilate could introduce him, but we know that he should have said 'Behold the truth'. In the opening lines of his work John has told us that Jesus is the Word made flesh 'full of grace and truth' (John 1:14). He is full of the very nature of God, God's characteristics, his qualities. And so Jesus can say 'I am the … truth' (John 14:6). If you want to know what corresponds with the reality of God, then you must look at Jesus. If you want to know what God is like, what his character is, then you must get to know Jesus, the truth. Truth is not an abstract concept, nor just a disembodied characteristic, truth is a person, one person, Jesus Christ. Pilate is baffled, because truth is staring him in the face, and he refuses to consider truth's claim on himself. He can only ask the question, he is not prepared to answer it for himself.

The Balance of Truth

So what is truth? The Christian, biblical answer must begin with Jesus Christ, *the* truth. For Christians truth is not just to be found in rationality, in observation of objects and events, although it certainly is to be found there. But truth is also to be found in the character of God revealed in his Son, Jesus Christ. Christianity, therefore, is not just rational and proclamatory, it is personal and pastoral; it is not just concerned with minds, but with lives; its mission is not just to communicate true concepts, but to transform lives by and in the truth of God; Christianity knows the difference between a lecture and a sermon.

One young man in his mid-twenties gradually revealed to an older Christian with pastoral responsibility for him that he struggled with a homosexual orientation. As a Christian he had accepted that it would be wrong to enter into any kind of genital relationship with another man; he felt called at that time to celibacy, and had already found that liberating. But he still lived very much at the level of struggle with his sexuality. What brought him even greater liberation was the discovery, through the ministry of a range of Christians, that God the Father loved him profoundly and unconditionally. That love touched him so deeply that it seemed to fill a gaping void in his life, left by an upbringing in which love, and especially the love of a father, had been in very short supply. God moved very graciously in his life, firstly helping him to accept the truth of his moral standards as a clear framework for his life, and then touching him with the truth of his love at a deeply personal level. In his case this led to his being set free from homosexual feelings to experience a heterosexual orientation for the first time in his life.

We need, however, to beware of moving from the conviction that truth is more than external, more than the rational and conceptual, to the point where we give the impression that Christianity is nothing to do with the rational and conceptual, that Christian truth is purely a matter of emotion and feeling. We live in an age which is impatient with doctrine, and whose motto is 'How can it be wrong when it feels so right?' But that is a profoundly unchristian motto. God has revealed himself supremely in a person, and not in a concept, but we know of that person through the words of the biblical writers. So we believe that the truth which is a right reflection of reality, and the truth which is a profound feature of character, belong together. In the Christian life right understanding and changed lives belong together, the one profoundly affects the other, just as a perfectly true life and perfectly true teaching are found together in the Son of God.

It is an abiding feature of the Reformed, Evangelical tradition that these two expressions of truth are held together in balance. A true Christian is not just someone who knows right doctrine, but someone whose life has been changed through hearing it. A true Christian is not just someone who has good religious feelings, or who behaves in a certain way, but someone who knows the truth of God, someone who has been set free by that truth. That balance is finely expressed by the Dean of Christ Church, Oxford, during the period of the Commonwealth, that great pastor and theologian John Owen: 'Let us, then, not think that we are any thing the better for our conviction of the truths of the great doctrines of the Gospel ... unless we find the power of the truths abiding in our own hearts and have a continual experience of their necessity and excellency in our standing before God and our communion with him.' John Owen is concerned that people should not just be Protestant, but that they should be Evangelical, they should discover that the truth of Christ is good news, life-transforming good news.

If Christian pastoral work, then, is to be faithful to Christian theology, it must hold together a balance. Our concern as pastors, and as leaders of a pastoral community, is that people should *live* in the truth. A colleague returned home after a time working in an overseas church famed for its doctrinal orthodoxy. His comment was illuminating: 'I sometimes felt that every single person in that church could have written down concisely on one side of A4 an entirely orthodox statement of the doctrine of the atonement, but I did long for some of them sometimes to be able to say what it meant to be forgiven.' We are called to minister the whole of God's revealed truth to whole people, and not just to one part of them, be it their minds or bodies or feelings.

The Reality of Reality

There is a further element to be held in balance, and that is that we minister to people the truth of God in the reality of their environment. Here is another key point for Christian pastoral theology. We are not Platonists who believe that the true, the real is only found beyond this visible world in an *ideal* which is at present invisible. We are not Gnostics, the Platonists' bastard offspring, who believe that this world is positively evil, and must be escaped from if we are to know the truth of God. If Christianity begins with Jesus Christ, who both spoke the truth and *is* the truth, it also embraces the whole revelation of God in the Scriptures, which begin with the truth of God's creation. This world is not less than the best, it is certainly not evil, it is rather God's creation, 'and he saw that it was good'. And God is not just Creator, but also Sustainer (Isaiah 40:21–6; John 5:17; Hebrews 1:13); he not only sustains this world, but he delights in it, and loves it in spite of all that human beings do to spoil it (Proverbs 8:30–31; John 3:16).

This conviction of the reality of reality, based in the doctrine of creation, profoundly affects our Christian pastoral concern. We do not just have a falsely 'spiritual' ministry to people, but we minister to them spiritually in the reality of their reality. We take account of their inner reality, the complexity of each person's individual make-up, and of those realities that make up their exterior world, the environment of home, family history, social and national setting, church. We cannot separate people from that reality without doing violence to them, because physical reality is real, not something that can be dismissed as of lesser importance than what is unseen and spiritual.

A vital part of Christian pastoral ministry, then, is helping people to face up to the reality of reality; until we have done that, we cannot effectively apply to them the spiritual realities that we also want them to face up to.

Now, this might happen in a whole variety of ways. The new minister naturally spends time in getting to know the social setting of her or his parish or area. Walking the streets, talking to people of all kinds in the community, reading the local paper, listening to local radio are all important for the process of beginning a pastoral ministry. That is not just a practical necessity, it is an important theological statement of the reality of creation. The Eastern mystic or monk might seek to draw people out of the rottenness of the every-day by chanting repetitive mantras or reciting ancient liturgies; the Christian pastor is out there in people's own setting, affirming that, however much that setting may have been damaged by sin, it is still real and good because it is part of God's good creation, it is a place where God is still at work.

Taking a step forward in ministry to that real world may involve a pastor and congregation doing further research into the true nature of a parish or area. The concept of a 'parish audit' again affirms the reality of reality: we cannot escape the truth, the observable facts about the setting in which we are ministering. Such an audit involves surveying an area in order to get a true picture of the range of people who live in it, their social relationships and needs. It also involves a church looking clearly at its own gifts and resources, so that it is more aware of areas in which it can effectively minister to its locality. If you want to know more about 'Parish Audits', John Finney's *The Well Church Book*[2] is a useful resource to help you discover the reality of the reality in which your church is set.

As we come to understand the real setting of our church and its people we shall be renewed in our conviction that Christian preaching must be genuinely pastoral; in other words, it is less than biblical if it fails to apply the revealed truth of Scripture to the reality of reality in which the hearers live. Church is not an escape from the painfulness of reality, even though its ministry may well need to have a strong element of refreshing the weary; but Christian worship and fellowship offer refreshment by helping people to see God at work in the reality of their daily setting, by interpreting that setting in the light of the Bible, and by equipping God's people to serve him in that real setting. The acknowledgement of the truth of the creation is a vital first step in Christian pastoral thinking.

Much of our pastoral care will be amongst individuals who have a poor grasp of the reality of reality. The human mind seems to have an almost limitless ability to distort our perception of reality, and many people (including ministers!) live with such a distorted view. If we are to minister in a genuinely Christian way, then we must be ready to accompany them to the point where they can see reality. A woman in her seventies who has recently become a member of your church following the death of her husband never takes communion, even though she comes regularly to the Parish Communion service. One day she asks to come and see you, and explains that, at the age of 14, she copied the answers for a school exam from a friend's book; the guilt of that single episode has clung to her for sixty years; for a long time it has prevented her from coming to church at all, and now prevents her from coming to communion, even though she has been confirmed as a child and has now stepped back into the worshipping life of the Christian community. Her whole grasp of reality has been distorted by the memory of a single episode, which to most people would seem trivial, but which has marked her whole life. The aim of the Christian pastor and preacher is surely to bring her into the truth in two ways, firstly to help her understand the true nature of her feelings of guilt about this act, secondly to help her to understand the true nature of God's forgiveness. Helping her into this truth will also set her free to address other realities which she has not been able to consider because the school copying incident has crowded them out.

That may seem like a relatively straightforward case, but it is worth noting that I have twice used the word 'understand' in describing one's pastoral aims with the woman. One should beware of thinking that one can achieve one's pastoral goals simply by concentrating on the intellectual; the understanding that is necessary may well not come at a purely intellectual level. As Richard Sibbes, another great Puritan said, 'Religion is especially seated in the affections.'[3] And it is this woman's feelings, her affections, that need to be touched here as much as her mind. I think she needs to *feel* that she is forgiven; the story of the cheating needs to be listened to carefully. She needs to know that a fellow Christian accepts her, and can minister God's forgiveness to her; she needs to experience an accepting warmth that helps her to let go of her guilt to the Lord who died for her. For her to get past the blockage that has hindered her from growing as a Christian for so long, she needs to grasp the reality of her own action and the reality of God's forgiveness, not just with her mind, but with her whole being. Because she feels that she has offended a figure of authority, her school teacher, she may well need to hear the promise of forgiveness from a figure of similar authority, such as a minister. Pastoral conversation and prayer with her will also help to inform the pastor's preparation for preaching about forgiveness. We can never preach of forgiveness with cold logic; surely it must be preached with the passion that shows how we can experience forgiveness in a deeply personal fashion.

Cognitive-behavioural Counselling

Methods of counselling that are concerned with helping people to face up to the reality of reality are generally called 'cognitive-behavioural' methods. Roger Hurding sums up these methods well: 'Cognitive approaches to counselling argue that irrational beliefs need to be recognized and countered by more realistic assessments, so that negative behaviour gives way to more socially acceptable responses.'[4]

It is relatively easy to see how these methods of counselling can be used to good effect. Modern treatment of sex offenders relies heavily on cognitive behavioural counselling. Sex offenders almost invariably deny any responsibility for their actions at first; if they admit that they did something, they will tend to say that they were only doing something loving. There is a strange pecking order amongst sex offenders in prison – this one will claim that his actions were more loving than the other's. What appears to be the most effective treatment of sex offenders starts with ensuring that offenders accept that they really did commit acts; it then moves on to getting them to accept that what they did was wrong; the final stage is to show them that they can adopt new patterns of behaviour, they can walk past the children's playground, they can see their own children as something other than sex objects, they can treat women as human beings, they can escape from their own past, which has frequently been a cycle of sexual abuse. The process is carried through in a group setting, where no individual can get away with denying the reality of his actions or responsibility because the other members of the group will not allow him to do so.

Now there is much in this that will make sense to Christians. In Romans 12:2 Paul makes it clear that our whole lives will be transformed by the renewing of our *minds*; if our thinking is straight, our behaviour will be straight – Paul moves directly from the cognitive to the behavioural. Perhaps we should add that Paul does not understand 'mind' in a shallow sense, as simply what we think is right. In Romans 7 he has already shown that he knows how believers struggle with the gap between what they know is right and what they actually do. Paul's concern is that the way we think and understand in the depths of our being should be right before God. The Psalmist says the same thing in slightly more poetical form: 'I treasure your word in my heart, so that I may not sin against you' (Psalm 119:11). So we should not be surprised that some Christians have taken up cognitive-behavioural methods; the most prominent of these is undoubtedly Jay Adams, whose 'Christian counselling' looks suspiciously like the behaviourism of his teacher O. H. Mowrer, who was not a Christian, covered with a veneer of Christianity, a veneer so thin it is at times transparent. Adams believes the Christian counsellor's first duty is to ensure that the client is converted; when that conversion has taken place, one can move swiftly towards giving the client the sort of clear advice which will change whatever behaviour pattern is wrong, and enable the situation to move towards a solution.

Part 4 has a lot more to say about Adams, and I think it may be helpful to read it carefully; but let me make one or two key points here. The strength of Adams' work is his insistence that proclamation and counselling are connected; truth is not the province of one and not of the other. It must be present in both. There are, however, many weaknesses in Adams' work. Firstly he has a very one-dimensional view of Scripture; his model is the book of Proverbs, the giving of clear advice, but there is a lot more to Scripture than the book of Proverbs. Secondly this approach is good with selected behaviour, but it is bad with illness and with problems whose root lies outside the counsellee's own behaviour. Wrong behaviour may not be due to wrong perceptions, but rather to illness. The person we are dealing with may be damaged by the sins of others, and not just the victim of his or her own sins. Adams, however, seems at times to come close to rejecting the idea of mental illness, as his mentor Mowrer did. He also appears to reject any idea that a person's problems may be caused more by the sin of others than by her own sin. A key element of any counselling situation is trying to discern what one is dealing with: 'Whose problem is this? The person sitting in front of me's, or someone else's? Is this mental illness or not?' When a minister feels that he or she may be dealing with a situation which involves a very complex web of relationships, or mental illness, we must recognize that we are not equipped to deal with it and we must pass the person on to someone else. Adams does not seem to offer us any help in discerning such situations. Thirdly this approach is in danger of setting up strong exterior structures for people's lives by the giving of clear advice, without at the same time ensuring that people have truly accepted inner change, that people *want* to change in themselves. Counsellees – and all of us – gain more when we see truth ourselves than when we are told it by a counsellor or preacher.[5]

There is another major problem with the whole concept of cognitive-behavioural counselling. If the aim of the counselling is to help someone to grasp the truth, who is deciding what the truth is? This must be a matter of concern for Christians. The misuse of behavioural methods in psychiatry in the old Soviet Empire is so well-documented as to be known to everybody. Psychiatry, counselling was used to change the behaviour of people whose behaviour was wrong, i.e. it did not conform to Marxist-Leninist-Stalinist norms, the only truth recognized by the state. But there are many more subtle examples of counsellors' own preconceptions falsely colouring their work, even to the extent of turning people away from the reality of reality rather than helping them to face it. One of my colleagues, a clinical psychologist, points out that Freud for a long time refused to accept that women's stories of sexual abuse were true; his own preconceptions about fathers forced him to interpret those stories as fantasies of infantile sexuality. As a result, Freud failed many women clients, and left a malign legacy to the future of psychiatry that it has only recently been able to leave behind.

But is it not also possible for Christians to use theology in such a way that it refuses to accept the reality of reality? Adams' theological position does not really leave room for mental illness, and it underplays the importance of feelings. The result is that some people's reality will be denied. Many people simply do not operate on the level of rationality in their decision making, they make their decisions according to feelings. Some people's reality is not rational because their capacity for rationality has been damaged by mental illness. A middle-aged man once told me a lengthy and disturbing story about events from his childhood, in which one of my predecessors as vicar played a prominent part. What credence was I to give to his story? My opinion of his story changed when I discovered that the man had a long history of mental illness. That did not necessarily make his story untrue, but it did mean that I had to see him in a different light; part of my ministry to him was to ensure that he was receiving the proper treatment, and to talk to other family members to obtain their view of his story. To do otherwise would have been to let him down, to deny his real needs.

Other Christians will have such a strong theology of demons that they ascribe sin to demonic activity, and therefore both diminish an individual's responsibility, and advocate some quite inappropriate solution to the problem. When we lived in Central Africa we became quite annoyed with testimony sessions at which people repeatedly ascribed anything that went wrong to 'Satan'. They seemed often to be saying, either 'I am not responsible,' or, even more dangerously, 'God is not really sovereign over what happens in my life.' Yet other Christians may be so influenced by a rationalistic spirit that they fail to take seriously accounts of demonic activity, and start looking for some imaginary psychiatric problem when there is none present.

Christian theology can subtly undermine the reality of reality – 'but that can't have happened' actually means 'my theology won't allow me to admit that that happened.' There are well-documented instances of churches allowing leaders to continue sexually abusing children and adults because the general belief in the Christian community was that a trusted leader could not possibly be doing something like that, even though people were coming forward with evidence to the contrary. We need to be aware that we can fall into that danger of denying reality as easily as the next person. It may even be easier for us to do so if our theology does not enable us to take reality seriously. Christian theology can retreat into romanticism, which fails to recognize evil for what it is, or into asceticism, which fails to recognize good for what it is. As Christians we do have a perfect model of truth, of reality: the Lord Jesus Christ himself. He both assures us of the goodness and reality of God's creation, and points up the sinfulness of human beings within that creation. A theology which is true to him can never be a theology which denies the reality of reality, whether that reality be good or bad.

Notes

1. Owen, John, *Works*, XII:52
2. Finney, John, *The Well Church Book*, Warwick, CPAS, and London, Scripture Union, 1991
3. Sibbes, Richard, *Works*, VI, 520
4. Hurding, Roger, *The Bible and Counselling*, London, Hodder & Stoughton, 1992, p. 153
5. cf. Mills, L. O., 'Truth-telling', in Hunter, R. J., (Ed.), *Dictionary of Pastoral Care and Counselling*, Nashville, Abingdon, 1990, pp. 1288f.

EXPOUNDING THE
PASTORAL WORD

PAUL THE PASTOR

Perspectives on Pastoral Theology from the Corinthian Epistles

'There are many ways of using the New Testament ... Equally rewarding is to read it in light of the pastoral concerns of those in the early Church.' S. M. Gilmour[1]

The third part of this book is an attempt to do what I have been suggesting is possible and necessary for Christian pastoral practice, namely to expound the Bible as a pastoral document, in the light of pastoral experience. First I want to look at the Corinthian Epistles from a pastoral viewpoint, and to consider Paul as an exemplar of pastoral practice. One cannot, of course, simply read a pastoral theology off the pages of the Bible, Old or New Testament; the proper and painstaking hermeneutical task of 'merging the horizons' of the Bible's world and our own must be undertaken, and yet one should beware of overestimating the distance between the Bible, especially the New Testament, and ourselves. It is not simply that we can discover parallels between the situation at Corinth and our own contemporary situation,[2] we can also discover theological principles which are not historically or culturally relative and which affect Paul's pastoral practice and should affect ours too.

The Corinthian Epistles provide a useful starting point for the discovery of such principles, not only because this is Paul's most extensive surviving correspondence, but also because it is the most obviously *pastoral* example of his correspondence, dealing at some length with the pastoral needs of the Corinthian church. Doubtless Paul would not have understood his correspondence as pastoral in any one-dimensional sense. For him theology and ministry are thoroughly integrated, just as theology and ethics are.[3] In the Corinthian correspondence 'one sees both the profoundly "situational" character of his theology and the profoundly theological character of his ministry.'[4] Paul's situation is not the same as ours, but the very integration of his thinking helps to bridge the gap between him and us, because he shows us 'the indissoluble integrity of Gospel and mission, and ... how each defines and supports the other.'[5] Paul's Gospel is ours, and should define and support our mission.

One should also point out that the very word *pastoral* is not one that looms large in Paul's vocabulary. In fact, the word *poimen* is found in the Pauline corpus only at Ephesians 4:11, where it is closely linked with 'teachers', from which we can assume that Paul did not think of 'pastoral work' as some kind of activity separate from the rest of his ministry, or indeed the ministry of the churches which he founded and to which he wrote. The thoroughly integrated nature of Paul's thinking and writing in all his letters is perhaps the first point that we can apply to our own pastoral thinking. As Stephen Pattison points out, much modern writing about pastoral care makes it a highly specialized occupation, but for Paul pastoral care is part of ministry as a whole. We cannot separate out in Paul's thinking and practice different areas such as teaching, evangelism, leading worship or addressing problem areas. Paul does not see 'pastoral ministry' as a highly specialized task, it is one aspect of an integrated whole – is it in our own pastoral thinking?[6]

Paul's Relationship with the Corinthians

The Corinthian correspondence shows us that Paul was neither a hit-and-run evangelist, nor a fair-weather friend to the churches he had founded. The critical problems relating to the Corinthian correspondence may not prove to be easily soluble,[7] but they do show us that the two canonical letters were probably part of a much longer correspondence between Paul and the Corinthians, even if theories that 2 Corinthians in particular is an amalgam of various Pauline letters no longer seem to be much in fashion.[8] Not only did a variety of letters pass between Paul and the Corinthians over quite a long period, but the surviving correspondence shows us that there were several visits by members of Paul's mission team to Corinth, and by Corinthian Christians to Paul (see 1 Corinthians 1:11; 16:5–11,17; 2 Corinthians 7:6–7,13; 8:17; 12:18; 13:1). The ongoing close relationship of Paul and his mission team in the churches he founded, and especially the Corinthian church, appears to be unique in contemporary religious life and work.[9] This again emphasizes the integrated nature of Paul's thinking. He is not just an evangelist, he is also a pastor; his aim is not just to plant new churches and create new Christians around the Mediterranean, he is concerned also to nurture those communities in the faith, the Gospel which he preached to them in the first place. That Gospel of reconciliation will nurture them now, just as it brought them to faith in the first place (2 Corinthians 5:16–21). That Gospel has practical, pastoral implications (e.g. 1 Corinthians 6:15), and Paul is determined to take the time and effort necessary to spell out those practical demands.

Such a concern for ongoing relationships with the churches is not seen in the Corinthian correspondence alone: his earliest correspondence, with the Thessalonian church, is protracted; and, even when Paul is writing to churches which he has not founded, such as that in Rome, his letters show a clear grasp of their situations, and a considerable effort to grapple theologically with them. Whilst naturally Paul spent more time with some churches than others, the depth of his concern for the churches is always apparent: 'The power of what he said is not derived from his priority in time, but from his penetration into the theme.'[10]

Christ-centred Living

Anthony Thiselton has shown that Paul's aim in 1 Corinthians especially is to bring the Corinthians back from a false concentration on an 'over-realized eschatology' to a truly God-centred, Christ-centred faith with all its practical implications.[11] Thus the climax of

1 Corinthians is chapter 15, which simultaneously underlines the past reality of the resurrection of Christ as the heart of the Gospel, and the future resurrection of believers in Christ. Equally richly christological is 2 Corinthians, 'for we do not proclaim ourselves; we proclaim Jesus Christ as Lord, and ourselves as your slaves for Jesus' sake' (2 Corinthians 4:5). Christ is not only the content of Paul's ministry, but also the motive for that ministry, as he must be for the ministry of the Corinthians (2 Corinthians 8:9). Paul does not see Christ as in any way unconnected with God the Father, or indeed the Holy Spirit; they are often linked in the Corinthian correspondence (e.g. 1 Corinthians 1:3,9,24; 2:10; 12:4–6; 2 Corinthians 1:2,3,19; 3:17; 5:18–21; 13:14) but the emphasis is on Christ. The typically Pauline phrase 'in Christ' is constantly found in these letters. Paul's whole theology is Christ-centred, and so should ours be. This may appear at first sight to be stating the obvious, but much modern thinking about pastoral work appears to be centred on professional skills rather than on the only centre that Paul would recognize for any theology, which is Christ.

But Paul's Christ-centredness goes much deeper than simply a theological formulation, because the Corinthian correspondence shows us that Paul had begun to experience in his own life something of what Christ himself had experienced. In contrast to the Corinthians' claims that they had reached a present state of spiritual perfection which meant that they were beyond suffering and servanthood in this life (1 Corinthians 4:8) Paul emphasizes that a life lived for Christ will in fact involve weakness and suffering, because it will be a life lived in the light of the cross (1 Corinthians 4:10–13). That suffering has been the experience of all the apostolic band, but especially of Paul himself (2 Corinthians 11:23–12:10). It is precisely in this experience of weakness and suffering that Paul has discovered Christ's power (2 Corinthians 12:9). Paul is not just a preacher and teacher of the Gospel of Christ; he actually lives that Gospel, the Gospel of Christ crucified (1 Corinthians 1:23). It is not just Paul's thinking which is thoroughly integrated and Christ-centred; his daily life is integrated with his thinking, and in himself people can see Christ, the crucified (1 Corinthians 4:17).

If pastoral theology is to follow the Pauline model, it will concern itself not just with right, Christ-centred thinking, but with right, Christ-centred living. Paul, the pastor, lives his Christ-centred message, and expects his readers to do so also.

This helps to explain Paul's frequent calls in the Corinthian correspondence to imitate him; this is not an example of Pauline arrogance, but a concern to impress upon the Corinthians that they are called to follow Christ in this world on the way to the cross, and that they can see a living example of what that may involve in Paul himself. Hence Paul's plea in 1 Corinthians 4:16: 'I appeal to you, then, be imitators of me' follows immediately on his description of the apostles' suffering in verses 9–13. Paul is not just saying to the Corinthians that he himself had experienced failure, and that this is a vital Christian experience, as Pattison suggests in commenting on 2 Corinthians 4:8–10.[12] What Paul experienced was the 'failure' of Christ; he lived a life so Christ-centred that in it he even experienced the sufferings of Christ, and so his life became an example, a picture of Christ to others. In saying this, we should beware of portraying Paul as a great, suffering, individual saint; such an image could be a burden for people to attempt to imitate rather than an encouraging example. Paul's suffering is, at least in part, a sharing in the suffering of the whole Body of Christ. For a pastor to say to people 'I myself have failed' may be important, because it prevents the pastor being put on an unattainable pedestal; far more important is it that people see in the pastor – and, indeed, in the whole Body of Christ – an example of the cross. Failure is not necessarily a disaster for the Church, it may reflect the cross of Christ. The failing Church may be one which is truly Christ-centred.

Christ-centred Flexibility

If Paul's thinking and life are thoroughly Christ-centred, this does not mean that he writes to the Corinthians in a facile way. This Christ-centred thinker is extraordinarily flexible in his thinking and in his approach to the Corinthians. Because of his submission to

Christ, Paul sees himself not as lording it over the Corinthians, but rather as their servant 'for Jesus' sake' (2 Corinthians 4:5). And this stance of service shows itself in the way Paul writes to them. At first sight the Corinthian letters can seem rather disjointed, until one realizes that in them Paul is responding to points made by the Corinthians in their own letters and other communications. Thus on several occasions in 1 Corinthians Paul refers to some statement or question of the Corinthians, introduced by the phrase *peri de*, as at e.g. 1 Corinthians 7:1,25; 8:1. Almost certainly Paul also quotes the Corinthians elsewhere without using this introductory phrase, as for example at 1 Corinthians 6:12.

One possible explanation for the even more disjointed nature of 2 Corinthians is that Paul is responding to more questions from the Corinthians, some of which may have been reported to him during the actual course of writing the letter. It is not possible, of course, to reconstruct the exact series of events that lies behind the correspondence, but we can see how carefully Paul engages with the thinking and questions of the Corinthians. He starts where they are in their thinking and, by suggestion and qualification, brings them back to a more truly Christ-centred faith and way of life. Paul does not simply denounce their thinking as false, even if at times he does appear to be very angry with the Corinthians (e.g. 1 Corinthians 5:1–5). His first thoughts about them are positive (1 Corinthians 1:4–9; 2 Corinthians 1:7; 3:2–3), and he writes to them on the basis of what they are 'in Christ'.

Beginning from where the Corinthians are, Paul works through their questions and examines their situation in considerable theological depth. The disunity of the church, for instance, is not just due to the ministry of different Christian leaders – Apollos, Cephas, Paul himself – but results from a failure on the part of the Corinthians to grasp the message of the cross (1 Corinthians 1–3). This subtle theological analysis continues throughout the two letters; sometimes the subtlety might seem to cloud the meaning, as for example in 1 Corinthians 11:2–16, the notoriously difficult passage about women and veils, where Paul appears to be using four different interwoven arguments at once. This passage might, of course, seem clearer to us if we had access to the Corinthians' side of the argument. Elsewhere his thinking is much easier to follow. When dealing with the Corinthians' abuse of the Lord's Supper, Paul's clear Christ-centred, cross-centred theology analyses their situation as a failure to grasp the centrality of the cross (1 Corinthians 11:26). 'Paul saw clearly that in Corinth faith had been misunderstood as conveying new religious *privileges* and a new spiritual *status*, and that neither the radical nature of the gift nor the radical scope of the claim of the Gospel had been grasped.'[13] When discussing marriage in 1 Corinthians 7, Paul twice brings the Corinthians back to a saying of the Lord in verses 10 and 12, but when he has no such saying to offer, he refuses to invent one just to shortcut the argument, e.g. verse 25. In fact, the whole tone of the chapter is to calm down the Corinthians' enthusiasm, which had led them into an ascetic view of marriage, by subtle suggestion and questioning rather than by a heavy-handed exercise of authority. Again, in 2 Corinthians, Paul counteracts the Corinthians' tendency to boast of their spiritual experiences by 'boasting' of his own experience of suffering in chapters 11–12; there is undoubted passion in Paul's writing, but no big stick.

Paul is indeed 'all things to all people' (1 Corinthians 9:22) at Corinth, because he refuses to distance himself in any final way from the Corinthian church. He consistently aligns himself with their opinions (e.g. 1 Corinthians 8:1; 14:18) and then moves them on to see that there is a better way, the way of Christ, whose love took him to the cross (1 Corinthians 12:31). His flexibility is such that he is even ready to face accusations that he is elastic in his principles (2 Corinthians 1:13–24), and to lay himself open to misinterpretation. For example, it could be said that he supports the ascetic ideals in 1 Corinthians 7. But he will not take short cuts in dealing with the situation of the church in Corinth.[14] And yet he never merely reacts to the Corinthians' questions, developing his theology as he goes along; his thinking is always Christ-centred from the beginning, and he has a clear understanding of where he wants to lead the Corinthians. As Tidball points out, Paul's epistles are all pastoral, all bridge-building, but the meeting place is determined by the gospel-side of the bridge, because the Gospel of Christ crucified and risen is non-negotiable.[15] Paul's pastoral practice and theology is astonishingly subtle and flexible, but gloriously Christ-centred. Does our thinking and practice measure up to such a standard?

Authority and Community

Paul's understanding of his authority as a Christian leader stems from his understanding of his calling. It is not one that he has chosen for himself, in fact it often leads him into danger and suffering (2 Corinthians 6:4–10; 11:23–29), but he is under obligation to preach the Gospel (1 Corinthians 9:16), to preach the cross, the power of God displayed in Christ crucified (1 Corinthians 1:24). His desire is to please God, and he has been captured by the love of Christ (2 Corinthians 5:9,14). He knows also that he is under the judgement of God, both in the present and the future (1 Corinthians 3:11–15; 4:4–5; 15:10; 2 Corinthians 5:10–11). To sum up, all Paul's motivation derives from God in Christ.[16] This understanding of his calling and motivation profoundly affects Paul's understanding of his authority in relation to the Corinthian church. He sees himself as a servant of Christ, and therefore of the Corinthians (2 Corinthians 4:5; 1 Corinthians 3:5). Paul uses 'servant/slave' words to describe himself and his colleagues with striking regularity in both letters (1 Corinthians 4:1; 2 Corinthians 3:6; 4:5; 6:4; 11:23; cf. also 2 Corinthians 8:23), and his description of himself as sharing Christ's sufferings may allude to the Suffering Servant theme of Isaiah and Mark 10:45. Paul also uses 'family' words to describe his relationship with the Corinthians; he is their parent (1 Corinthians 4:14–15; 2 Corinthians 12:14), and their brother (1 Corinthians 1:26 *et passim*), because of what they all are in Christ. Paul has authority, but it is an authority in Christ, and therefore the model for his work is always Christ crucified, who shows how that authority is to be exercised. That is why, as we have already seen, Paul's concern is to draw out what the Corinthians already are in Christ, rather than to order them about so as to make them do what Paul wants.

This also affects Paul's understanding of the Christian community. He is not separate from the Christian community in Corinth, but a part of it in spite of his distance from them geographically, as his frequent use of 'brothers and sisters' indicates. And he insists that the Corinthians see themselves as members of a community, they are 'one body in Christ' (1 Corinthians 12). *All* have gifts within that body (1 Corinthians 12:7), and the essential pastoral task of building up the body is the responsibility of *all* and to be carried out for the benefit of *all* (1 Corinthians 12:14–25).

There can be no division within that body on the basis of gifts possessed, nor indeed on any special basis: in both Corinthian epistles Paul shows a particular concern for the poor, who were obviously in danger of being squeezed out of the fellowship of the Christian body (1 Corinthians 1:26–29; 11:22; 2 Corinthians 8–9). Paul consistently plays down individual status and gifts, in order to emphasize the corporate nature of the Christian life, in which all have a contribution to make. This is not just a matter of theological theory for Paul; he shows it in practice by his willingness to work with others, both in his own mission team (e.g. 1 Corinthians 16:10; 2 Corinthians 8:23), and in the Corinthian church (e.g. 1 Corinthians 16:15–18), and in his recognition of the gifts of other Christian leaders (1 Corinthians 3:5–6).

Paul's own gifts were clearly of an extraordinary nature, but he seems always to have used them in full awareness of the gifts of others, and of his own position as a servant of Christ. We should perhaps disabuse ourselves of any temptation to see Paul as a solitary colossus striding across the Mediterranean world on evangelistic missions. We know that he had enormous theological ability, but our detailed concentration on his theology and practice should not make us forget that he worked with a number of co-workers, and for the increasingly complex Christian communities which sprang from his own and others' mission. His whole understanding of his work is formed from his prior understanding of what it means to be *in Christ*. He would certainly not see his pastoral task as the kind of 'one-to-one' involvement which is often the model for pastoral care today, nor would he see pastoral theology as simply concerning itself with the solving of problems for people, nor indeed would he see himself as *the* pastor over against the rest of the church. Paul's concern is with the life of the Body of Christ, and with building up that body in Christ.[17] Any attempt to build a pastoral theology on biblical foundations must take this corporate concern of Paul's very seriously.

Images of Ministry

Whilst most of this chapter has been given over to considering the principles which seem to underlie and mould Paul's pastoral practice and thinking, it may also be worthwhile to consider rather more briefly another way in which the Bible has often been used in pastoral theology. Pastoral theologians have often turned to the Bible, especially the Pauline corpus, as a source of images of the pastoral task. A recent example of such a use of biblical images can be found in Alistair V. Campbell's *Rediscovering Pastoral Care*.[18] We need to examine whether these images are used by pastoral theologians with due respect for the theological context in which they are originally to be found. Paul's Corinthian correspondence is certainly not lacking in such images, as Paul attempts both to explain his own work and to encourage the Corinthians to serve Christ faithfully in their own situation. Tidball, without claiming that his list is exhaustive, mentions fourteen such images in the Pauline corpus,[19] and nine of these occur in the Corinthian letters. It might be instructive to concentrate here on four of those images which seem especially important both to Paul and in modern pastoral thinking.

(i) **Family images**: We have already seen how often Paul describes himself as either a parent or a brother to the Corinthians, and that this is an indication of his understanding of his own authority. It should be mentioned here that Paul's model is not that of a parent with small children, but of a parent with adult children, who are not to be shamed, but can responsibly accept a warning (1 Corinthians 4:14–15), and can make up their own minds as to what it means to be one of Paul's children when they shortly meet his other son,

Timothy (1 Corinthians 4:17). The picture in 2 Corinthians 12:14 also seems to portray a parent providing adult children with the means to make their way in life. The parent image further suggests the idea of helping children to grow up into maturity; that is certainly the image at 1 Corinthians 3:1–2, which is perhaps closer to the nursing mother image of 1 Thessalonians 2:7, where the picture is of small children. That theme of helping the Corinthians grow into maturity is developed throughout the rest of 1 Corinthians 3, where we find the second image I want to discuss here.

(ii) **The Builder**: Paul frequently uses the *oikodomeo* word group in the Corinthian correspondence, not only in the very obvious images of 1 Corinthians 3, but especially in 1 Corinthians 14, when reminding the Corinthians that they must seek for gifts that will build up the whole Body of Christ. Those gifts must be used in love (1 Corinthians 13), because only love builds up (1 Corinthians 8:1). What builds up is an attitude of seeking the good of others (1 Corinthians 10:23–24). Again in 2 Corinthians Paul uses the image of building in describing his own ministry (2 Corinthians 10:8; 12:19; 13:10) and to remind the Corinthians of their Christian hope (2 Corinthians 5:1). We must build now in hope of the building which God has prepared for us in the future.

Paul's frequent use of this image should again remind us that the first task in pastoral work is not the resolution of individuals' problems, but the positive building up of the whole Body of Christ. The Body must be built up not just so that it runs as smoothly as possible, but so that it can be an effective witness to the world around (1 Corinthians 5:9–10; 14:23–25).

(iii) **The Fool**: The image of the fool seems to delight some modern writers on pastoral care,[20] and it is certainly used by Paul in 1 Corinthians 1–3 with some frequency. But we should perhaps beware of an overly simple use of the word 'fool', which takes no account of the biblical background. In the Old Testament, a 'fool' is not just someone who makes others laugh, nor just someone suffering from mental illness or handicap. In passages such as Deuteronomy 32:6,

Isaiah 32:5f., 'foolishness is not lack of knowledge but rebellion against God.'[21] To be a fool is to turn directly against God, and that is surely the background to Paul's use of the idea of foolishness in 1 Corinthians. As far as his opponents are concerned, what Paul is saying is the complete opposite of the truth of God. But Paul stands firm in the foolishness of the cross. God's message, God's work, is indeed the complete opposite of what the world assumes it to be, it is the message of a crucified Messiah. The foolishness of Christian pastoral work is not just having a sense of humour, but of taking a stand against the false ideas of popular (folk?) religion and pointing people to Christ, who overturns all those false ideas.

(iv) **The Wounded Healer**: Another image of the pastor popular in contemporary thinking is that of the Wounded Healer.[22] It should perhaps be noted that the phrase 'the Wounded Healer' is not a scriptural one, although it is undoubtedly influenced by the language of Isaiah 53; it seems to originate with T. S. Eliot (*East Coker, 4*). Paul undoubtedly describes his own sufferings in the Corinthian correspondence, but the value of that suffering for him lies, as we have already seen, not in the suffering itself, but in suffering for and with Christ. If Paul heard the phrase 'Wounded Healer', he would, I suggest, think it applied to Christ himself. Paul was wounded because he was in Christ and so became an imitator of Christ to others. The Wounded Healer could be a misleading image for Christian pastoral work unless it is clearly seen in terms of our relationship with Christ; the suffering involved in ministry is an aspect of Paul's Christ-centred life and thought.

Paul's Pastoral Theology and Ours

It should be clear by now that Paul does not have a pastoral theology, because his thinking is not divided up into separate boxes marked 'doctrine' or 'ethics' or 'pastoral theology'. Theology and Christian life and work are all part of one whole, and at the centre of that one whole is Christ. There is much in Paul's Corinthian correspondence which might help us today in the task of creating a genuinely Christian pastoral theology, but we shall only succeed in that task if we see it as part of the whole theological task, and if our lives and thinking are centred in Christ.

Notes

1. Gilmour, S. M., 'Pastoral Care in the New Testament Church', *New Testament Studies*, 10:3, p. 398

2. As Graham Leonard does in *God Alive, Priorities in Pastoral Theology*, London, DLT, 1981, chapter 1

3. Furnish, V. P., in Shelp, E. E. and Sutherland, R., (Eds), *A Biblical basis for Ministry*, Philadelphia, Westminster, 1981, pp. 101–44

4. ibid., p. 102

5. ibid., p. 105

6. cf. Pattison, op. cit., chapters 1 and 2

7. cf. Barrett, C. K., *The Second Epistle to the Corinthians*, London, A. & C. Black, 1973, pp. 23ff.

8. cf. Hall, D. R., 'Pauline Church Discipline' in *Tyndale Bulletin* 20, 1969, pp. 3–26, who defends the unity of 2 Corinthians, in part, on a consideration of Paul's *pastoral* approach

9. Banks, Robert, *Paul's Idea of Community*, Exeter, Paternoster, 1980, p. 169

10. Keck, L. E. in Browning, Don S., (Ed.), *Practical Theology*, San Francisco, Harper and Row, 1983, p. 145

11. Thiselton, Anthony, 'Realized Eschatology at Corinth', *New Testament Studies*, 24, pp. 510–26

12. Pattison, op. cit., pp. 159f.

13. Furnish, op. cit., p. 139

14. Chadwick, H., 'All Things To All Men – 1 Corinthians 9:22', *New Testament Studies*, 1:4, pp. 261–75

15. Tidball, *Skilful Shepherds*, p. 100

16. ibid., pp. 102–3

17. cf. Pattison, op. cit., chapter 1

18. Campbell, Alistair V., *Rediscovering Pastoral Care*, London, DLT, 2nd ed., 1986
19. op. cit., pp. 104–11
20. cf. Campbell, op. cit., chapter 5; Pattison, op. cit., chapter 8; also Saward, John, *Holy Fools*, Oxford, OUP, 1980, chapter 1
21. Goetzmann, J., in Brown, C., (Ed.), *New International Dictionary of New Testament Theology*, Vol. 3, Exeter, Paternoster, ET, 1978, p. 1025. cf. also Bertram, G., in Kittel, G. and Friedrich, G. (Eds), *Theological Dictionary of the New Testament*, Vol. 4, Grand Rapids, Eerdmans, ET, 1967, pp. 832–47
22. The title of a book by Henry Nouwen, New York, Doubleday, 1972. See Campbell, op. cit., chapter 4; Pattison, op. cit., chapter 7

GOD THE PASTOR

The Book of Jeremiah as Pastoral Theology

Paul's Corinthian correspondence offers us one way into a pastoral interpretation of Scripture, beginning from the examples of pastoral work that we find within its pages. However, we are always aware that there is a gap between Paul's situation and our own, and we know that we need to seek not just patterns of pastoral practice that we can replicate, but deeper theological principles that can direct appropriate styles of pastoral work today. We need, in fact, to know more about God, to go deeper into his character and work, if our pastoral practice is to be true to the revelation in the Bible. To discover the character of God drives us not only to the New Testament, but also to the Old Testament, because that is the foundation for the New. The New Testament knows the character of God because it knows the Old Testament.

However, we have to say that looking to the Old Testament as a source for contemporary pastoral theology is not a very obvious thing to do; we are, after all, temporally and culturally far more distant from our forebears in ancient Israel than from those in first-century Corinth. Works of pastoral theology, as a result, tend to pay scant attention to the Old Testament. R. S. Anderson's weighty, strongly Barthian collection of pastoral theology, for example, fails to include a single article on the Old Testament amongst the twenty-eight gathered there, and covering nearly eight hundred pages.[1] Where attempts have been made to develop a pastoral perspective from the Old Testament, the attention has tended to be on the

Wisdom literature, either on the Psalms or the book of Job as examples of the individual's suffering and relationship to God, or, as Jay
Adams does, on Proverbs as a model for the giving of pastoral advice
in so-called Christian counselling. Those attempts are undoubtedly
valid, but they can and do give a false impression of the breadth of
the Old Testament's understanding of the pastoral task, and
contribute to the unhealthy individualistic stance of much modern
writing on pastoral care, both from evangelical sources and others.
Even more seriously, they fail to acknowledge the essential contribution the Old Testament must make to pastoral theology, simply
because it makes an essential contribution to *all* Christian theology.

We need, therefore, to take a wider look at the Old Testament if
we are to claim that our pastoral theology and practice is genuinely
biblical. After all the pastor/shepherd image itself is derived from
the Old Testament. But our concern is not just with images of
ministry to be found in the pages of the Bible. Our concern is with
the theological undergirding of all our faith and practice. That
concern needs to recognize something of vital importance, which is
that the whole of the Old Testament, and, indeed, the New
Testament, is *practical* theology, applied theology, pastoral theology.
The Bible knows nothing of academic theology; the different books
of the Bible arise out of quite specific practical situations, even if we
cannot always recreate those situations with any degree of accuracy.
Pastoral theology is a thoroughly biblical, central part of theology,
because the Bible itself is pastoral theology, not simply the New
Testament, but also the Old. The Old Testament is the basis of
Jesus' theology, and the New Testament's theology, and therefore of
the Christian Church's theology. So why should it not play its full
part in the Christian Church's pastoral theology, as long as it is
rightly interpreted and carefully applied?

What I want to do in this chapter, then, is to look at the book of
Jeremiah as pastoral theology. Why Jeremiah? First, because Jeremiah
occupies a central place in Old Testament thought and history. He is
the heir of the Law, especially Deuteronomy, of the eighth-century
prophets, and of the Wisdom tradition. Holladay's recent vast
commentary has shown the richness of theological influences on

Jeremiah.² Jeremiah also prepares the ground for the exilic and post-exilic prophets and for much later Wisdom writing, and is widely alluded to in the New Testament. In addition, of course, Jeremiah lived through a crucial period of Israel's history, which included both the revival under Josiah and the national, personal and *theological* disaster of the Babylonian invasions and exiles.

Secondly, the book of Jeremiah presents fewer critical problems than many of the other prophetic books, such as Isaiah. This is not to say that there is no critical work to be done in studying Jeremiah, or that critical questions have robbed other prophetic books of their value – they have not – but we can assert with some confidence that we are in direct touch with Jeremiah himself and his message, without having to wade through a vast amount of critical material that may not always be very edifying. However, there is one impor-tant critical question that we need to be aware of. Much of the crit-ical work on Jeremiah is concerned with the order of the book and the prophecies it contains: what did Jeremiah say when? Our book of Jeremiah is in some ways a bit of a mess as regards historical order, and as a result it does not really lend itself to *consecutive* exposition. This exposition, then, will be thematic rather than consecutive in its approach to the book, although we shall doubtless need to linger a little over some particular passages. What follows should not be regarded as a definitive commentary on Jeremiah.

Thirdly, Jeremiah is himself a pastor; he actually describes himself as a 'shepherd' in 17:16, and indeed a shepherd who has not run away from God's call. He is a godly leader for Israel. He was not alone in that pastoral role. Zephaniah, who seems to have had royal connections as opposed to Jeremiah's priestly connections, prophe-sied at roughly the same time as Jeremiah, although not over such a long period, and the book of Jeremiah itself tells us of another true prophet, Uriah, and also of godly political leaders in Israel (26:16–24). The Old Testament will not, of course, allow any neat division between religious and national leadership, pastoral and political roles; the image of 'shepherd' seems to be applied in the first place to kings in Israel (Ezekiel 34). So not only were others called to pastoral roles in Jeremiah's time, but his own pastoral role is also never an individualistic one. He lives and ministers as a shepherd in the context of the life of God's people, and indeed in the wider context of God's world, as we shall see later. And, most importantly, Jeremiah's ministry is derived from God's ministry; that is supremely the context in which he works,[3] and in which we must all work. The book of Jeremiah is not just the story of what Jeremiah said and did; it is concerned with what God says and does at a time of critical importance for the whole of Israelite and biblical history.

This chapter therefore will concern itself not so much with Jeremiah as an exemplar of pastoral practice, as with the book of Jeremiah's picture of God, who is himself shepherding Israel through an era of confusion and catastrophe. We are more concerned with God the pastor than Jeremiah the pastor. Nevertheless, the opening of the book shows us God focusing on Jeremiah, and, if we are to be true to that, we must start by thinking about God and Jeremiah himself.

God and Jeremiah

God works in and through people; that is basic to the theology of the whole Bible, it is incarnational theology, because at the heart of it is one *person* in whom God works supremely. But God prepares for his work in that one person by working in the whole of his people and his world. So the Bible is the story of God's work in the creation and in the people of Israel, and in certain individuals and their part within the story of the whole people – patriarchs, priests, prophets, kings, wise men. God's work in and through a prophet is regularly summed up in the account of that prophet's call; this is true of both the former prophets, for example, 1 Samuel 3, and the writing prophets, Isaiah 6:1–10; Ezekiel 1–3; Amos 7:14–15. In the writing prophets we do not always find the account of their call set out in formal fashion at the beginning of the written edition of their prophecies, but Jeremiah's call, like Ezekiel's and (in a very strange way) Hosea's, does form the introduction to the written collection of his prophecies in 1:1–19. This is perhaps because his call sums up what God is going to do through him even more clearly than is the case for some of the other prophets. So let us now concentrate on Jeremiah's call in chapter 1 as a way in to considering how God works in Jeremiah throughout his ministry.

Jeremiah's call is personal but not individualistic. In chapter 1 verses 4–5a emphasize the strongly personal nature of God's setting apart of Jeremiah – 'Before I formed you in the womb I knew you' – but we have already been made aware of the wider context in which he worked by the editor's historical introduction in verses 1–3. That wider context is underlined as the nature of the call unfolds in verses 5b, 9–10, 13–16 – '... a prophet to the nations ... I appoint you over nations and over kingdoms ... I will utter my judgements against them [i.e. all the inhabitants of the land].' This all prepares us for what is to follow. It prepares us for the structure of the book itself, in which Jeremiah's prophecies to the nation, and his very personal prayers, mainly in verse, are interwoven with historical passages, mainly in prose, which tell us something of his personal history in the context of the wider history of Israel and the surrounding world. It also prepares us for the book's portrayal of what is involved for Jeremiah in being a prophet, the personal cost of being God's prophet, as well as its record of his preaching to Israel. At the same time the mention of the nations reminds us that the book holds together not just prophecies concerning the nation of Israel but also others concerning the other nations of the ancient Near Eastern world. God works in Jeremiah as an individual, but he never works in him individualistically; rather he works through him to minister to the nation, his people, and to the world, his creation.

Jeremiah's call is also to share in God's work of judgement and re-creation. If he is 'to pluck up and to pull down, to destroy and overthrow', he is also 'to build and to plant' (verse 10). This again prepares us for what we shall see of Jeremiah's task in the rest of the book, which consistently interweaves themes of judgement and hope. Jeremiah is called to live out God's judgement and re-creation in his own life; Jeremiah has to live out God's comfort of the afflicted and his affliction of the comfortable. There are several examples in the book of prophetic actions and experiences which exemplify God's message. In perhaps the most demanding of all of

these Jeremiah is called to remain celibate as a sign of Israel's aloneness and devastation under judgement (16:1–4). In a more famous
passage we hear how, at the height of the Babylonian siege of
Jerusalem, God calls Jeremiah to buy a field as a sign of hope
(32:1–15) – and we are all aware that the property market is
frequently used as a marker for economic hopes; God obviously
thinks so too! We can perhaps also see how Jeremiah experiences in
himself God's work of judgement and re-creation in the treatment
he receives from others. As a result of his preaching he is persecuted
(e.g. 38:1–6), but also respected, even, grudgingly, by the notoriously inconstant King Zedekiah himself (38:7–28).

As Jeremiah's call involves his experiencing in himself God's
judgement and re-creation, so it is a *call to joy and suffering*
(1:17–18). God is with him to equip him for his task, but that task is
very demanding (verse 19). Jeremiah is not, of course, the only
prophet whose ministry led to his own suffering, but the experience
and depth of suffering is particularly marked in his case; there are
numerous accounts of Jeremiah's suffering in both the prose and
poetry of the book (e.g. 12:6; 15:15–18; 18:18). And yet he knew
God's grace and protection in a particularly marked fashion as well;
his apparently paradoxical experience is summed up in 15:15–16. In
human terms Jeremiah could be counted a failure, and yet God
accepts that failure, because Jeremiah's suffering reflects God's own
pain in the face of his people's disobedience and unwillingness to
accept his call to repentance. The account of Jeremiah's suffering in
11:18–23 is followed by Jeremiah's own complaint in 12:1–4, and
then by God's answer in 12:5–13, which shows his pain at his
people's abandonment of him. 'Prophetic suffering provides a deep
insight into the nature of Yahweh.'[4] We shall take a closer look at the
idea of failure in the next section.

So *Jeremiah's call demands obedience, but also provokes argument*
(1:6–7). The demands of God's call are such that, from the very
beginning, Jeremiah argues with God about it. And this arguing with
God, or 'confessions', is a very significant feature of the book of
Jeremiah (e.g. 17:14–18; 18:19–23; 20:7–18). At one point the
arguing becomes positively sinful, and God has to call Jeremiah to

repentance (15:15–19), but Jeremiah's experience shows us that God is ready for his arguing, he does not reject it; he is a God who is prepared to be argued with as he does his pastoral work in his people. At the same time God's readiness to listen to our arguing does not mean that he is morally indifferent. Jeremiah argues and is heard, but at times there is a sinful element in his arguing, and God does not ignore that. Pastoral ministry which truly reflects God's own nature and ministry will in some way reflect that perfect balance in God himself: a perfect readiness to listen and to be argued with, matched by a perfect moral righteousness. How easily our pastoral ministry loses that balance; we need to remember that God's pastoral ministry never does.

The account of Jeremiah's call and ministry tells us about far more than simply Jeremiah's own history. It illuminates for us what God expects of those called to a specific pastoral role, his call which is personal but never individualistic, his call to share in his own work of judgement and re-creation, his call to joy and suffering, his call that demands obedience but also provokes argument, and it also offers us a wider picture of the pastoral nature of God himself. In his own life Jeremiah experienced God's work of pastoral leadership, and that is why his prophetic ministry helps lay foundations for our own pastoral theology and ministry. It is not so much that we have to do exactly what Jeremiah did, of course we do not, because we live in a very different context; but we do have to do with the same God, the same Lord who is our shepherd, our pastor. Our pastoral ministry derives from him, it is a sharing in his work in the Church and the world, not our doing something that we think he might approve of; in New Testament terms it is a ministry 'in Christ Jesus' and not just for Christ Jesus. We are caught up, taken hold of by God to be his servants, to model ourselves on him and his pastoral ministry, and that is daunting; it was daunting for Jeremiah because it involved a very demanding call. But because it is God's ministry and his call, we can hear exactly what Jeremiah heard from the shepherd Lord: 'They will fight against you; but they shall not prevail against you, for I am with you, says the Lord, to deliver you' (1:19).

God and Failure

Readers may find it depressing to consider failure; many pastors are acutely aware of failure in their own ministry. But we do find failure in the Bible: the failure of God's people, the failure of their ministry, the failure to be what God wants his people to be, and especially the failure to achieve what we think we ought to. Christians have not normally found any difficulty in dealing theologically with the first kind of failure, the failure to be what God wants us to be; we do not find too much difficulty in talking about sin, repentance, forgiveness and transformation in Christ. But I suspect we are not so good at grappling theologically with the second kind of failure, the failure to achieve what we ought to. But we certainly do need to grapple with it. After all, those of us who live in western Europe at the end of the twentieth century live in a nation and a continent where God's people have failed. Our continent has moved away from being the centre of Christendom to a kind of neo-paganism and pluralism. As Lesslie Newbigin keeps on pointing out to us, Christianity is no longer seen as an option except of the 'Pick & Mix' variety, one of a whole range of personal philosophies which we are free to choose as we exercise our right to the 'pursuit of happiness'.[5] And we cannot say that this all results from the first kind of failure on the part of the Christian Church, the failure to be what God wants us to be. We cannot put it all down to unconfessed, unforgiven sin on our part, even though there is much in our failure that should drive us to repentance. The Church in Europe is, in many ways, holier, livelier and truer than it has been for many years, and yet we are failing to achieve what we ought to.

Within that wider context of the failure of the people of God in western Europe at the end of the twentieth century, I think we also need to see that our own ministry will often fail. One of the most stimulating things I do in my present job is to be involved in the supervision of ordinands on practical, pastoral placements. It is stimulating because that is a key time of trying to set up a conversation between what people are learning theologically and what they are experiencing in practical, pastoral ministry. One week our supervision group had to deal with a great deal of apparent failure as we discussed people's experience of training for hospital chaplaincy. Students had gone into this training opportunity with a burning desire to get alongside people and show them the love of God, and to share with them the reality of the Christian good news, and everyone felt that they had failed to achieve that. And there will be times, perhaps many times, when those of us in pastoral ministry will discover that our ministry is not working, but is failing. People are not responding to the Gospel even though we preach it faithfully, people are not in practice changing in a gospel fashion even though they appear to make a mental response to the Gospel, the Church is not able to penetrate the very tough hide of secularism which envelops our communities. And there will be moments when we shall wonder why we ever bothered getting into this ministry, whether anybody really appreciates what we are doing, and certainly why other people's ministry seems so much more successful than our own. We have to face up to failure in the Church and in our own ministry.

In Britain ministers of different denominations are normally trained in places associated with success, colleges attached to universities, which speak of academic achievement and rewarding job opportunities. Training for pastoral ministry is tied to university courses; success in gaining the appropriate diploma or degree becomes the final hurdle to be jumped before ordination itself. But does our association with success prevent our getting to grips with failure, the failure of the Church and our own potential failure?

And, because we are associated with success, are we able to minister to people who feel that they themselves are failures? We meet many people in that situation, both inside our congregations and outside – the divorced man who feels he has failed as a father, the unemployed who feel they are useless failures because no one wants to employ them, the grieving relatives who can only keep on repeating the ways in which they let down the one they are mourning, many women who have been brought up to believe that their gifts and talents are not needed just because they are women, the shy person who sits at the back of church each Sunday and feels a failure because he can't get up to the front and do all the exciting things other, successful Christians do. My own experience of pastoral ministry in the Church of England has been challenged by the realization that many people who themselves feel failures find that the average Anglican clergyman, with what a Catholic friend of mine called a typically Anglican effortless superiority, cannot relate to their failure. But we do meet with failure whether we like it or not; we meet it in others, but not only in others, for we also meet it in ourselves and in the Church that we serve.

Failure is an important theme for my own current work, and I think it is an important theme for all involved in the pastoral task. And we are not left completely in the dark when we consider failure from a Christian point of view, because failure is a theme that keeps recurring in the Bible. Job is a book not just about suffering, but about failure; King Saul is a classic example of someone who fails, and who is also overwhelmed by the success of someone else – David; and Ruth and Naomi are very ordinary people whose lives are blighted by failure. And then, of course, there is Jeremiah.

Jeremiah's Failure

Jeremiah failed. There is, I suppose, no more striking image of failure in the Bible than that description of King Jehoiakim burning Jeremiah's scroll; it is so cold and unemotional (36:23–24); Jeremiah has failed, he has nothing to say to us, and his words go up in smoke. And that is not the only example of Jeremiah's failure to get through to the people he was meant to get through to; they are quite determined not to listen to what he has to say, even if it means ridiculing him by putting him in the stocks (20:1ff.), or threatening him with death (chapter 26), or throwing him into a disgusting old cistern as a makeshift dungeon (chapter 38). His failure to be heard is summed up by the attitude of King Zedekiah and his court in 37:2.

But Jeremiah did not just fail, he was very well aware of his failure, the very depth of his being was scarred by it. The stirring, demanding call he had received in chapter 1 appears to come to nothing, and Jeremiah knows it – 'To whom shall I speak and give warning, that they may hear? See, their ears are closed, they cannot listen. The word of the Lord is to them an object of scorn; they take no pleasure in it' (6:10). The contrast between Jeremiah's sense of failure there and his calling in chapter 1 is immense. And his natural reaction is to run away, and get shot of it all — 'O that I had in the desert a traveller's lodging place, that I might leave my people and go away from them' (9:2). This is what psychologists call the flight reaction to failure and conflict. But, of course, the opposite reaction to flight is fight, and, even though Jeremiah toys with flight, in fact he stays to fight. Quite consistently he stays in the conflict situation, obedient to God's call. He could have gone off into exile along with many of the cream of the nation, the people who were in fact the good figs in the vision God gave him of the meaning of the exile, but he knew he had to stay with the bad figs and continue his ministry amongst them (40:1–6). In fact he ends up being kidnapped and taken off to Egypt, in clear disobedience to the command God had given through him. You have to stay and fight, running away achieves nothing.

Fighting with God

But Jeremiah did not just stay to fight with the situation and the people of Judah, he took his fight to God, he took his failure to God. And those passages known as the confessions of Jeremiah are key to understanding how we can deal with failure as the people of God. Firstly, Jeremiah is very direct with God; he hides nothing of his experiences or his feelings from God, because, as we have already noted in looking at the story of his call in chapter 1, he knows that God can cope with his arguing (17:15–16; 18:19). That simple directness is intense enough, but his prayer goes further than that, because Jeremiah is prepared not just to be open with God about what is going on, but to argue with him about the justice of the whole situation. We might paraphrase Jeremiah's prayer in 18:20 as 'God, if you were really just, if you were really in charge, then you'd do something about this situation.' That prayer becomes even more direct and demanding as it develops in verses 21–23. Now this really is becoming intense prayer, because the next stage is that Jeremiah begins to think the unthinkable, to pray the unprayable – 'Is it not just that I have failed, has God failed?' That may seem heretical, but it is there in Jeremiah, it is there in his prayers in 4:10; 8:19a. And God himself admits that he has failed – 'In vain I have struck down your children; they accepted no correction' (2:30a). In the face of failure prayer has to go very deep, it has to grapple with the very nature of God.

And that is what is happening here; we are not just grappling with Jeremiah and his failure, we are grappling with the very nature of God. Remember that quotation: 'Prophetic suffering provides a deep insight into the nature of Yahweh.' That is what is going on here, we are touching something of the depths in the nature of God himself. Jeremiah's experience of failure as a prophet was not just a personal disaster, Israel's experience of conquest and exile was not just a national disaster, what we have here is a theological disaster. A man and a nation are having their whole understanding of what God is like unpicked. But if it is being unpicked, something better is being recreated out of the pieces.

God's people have been living in a success culture of their own creation. They have only had to say their key words – 'The Temple of the Lord ... the Ark of the Covenant ... We are the circumcised' – and somehow success is guaranteed (7:1ff.; 3:16; 9:25–26). But that culture has trivialized the very nature of God, and they have to discover something of his real nature by going through the failure of exile. Because, in fact, what looks like God's failure is God's answer. God is not absent from the exile, but in it – that is the point of Jeremiah's famous letter to the exiles in chapter 29, which we consider more closely later. 'I have sent you into exile,' says God in 29:7; it is not a mistake, it is deliberate. God is in it, but in order to see that God is in it you need to start asking the really difficult questions, such as 'Has God failed?' If you just moan about the disaster, or simply try to smooth it all over as Jeremiah's false opponents did (e.g. Hananiah in chapter 28), then you understand nothing about the meaning of failure, and nothing about the nature of God. When you begin to see God *in* the failure, then you have real insight, prophetic insight.

Jeremiah is learning something else that is very important about the meaning of his own personal failure, his own failure as a prophet and pastor, as he keeps on arguing with God. He is learning that his personal failure in some way reflects the failure of the whole of God's people. In his prayer in chapter 8 he first of all brings to God the feelings of the people (verses 18–20), but then realizes as he prays that his own sufferings, his own failure, is somehow a reflection of the failure of God's people (verses 21–22). In the prayer in chapter 14 we see him able to confess the sins of the people; he knows that he is bound up inextricably with the whole life of the people, and that includes their failure and sin, and so he has to confess sin on their behalf. His prayer is not 'I', but 'we', the 'we' who are the whole people of God, past and present (verses 19–22). Just like Nehemiah and Daniel when they realized they had to confess the people's sins, Jeremiah lives out the truth that Paul had to live out in his pastoral ministry, that his own pastoral experience was inherently corporate: 'Who is weak, and I am not weak? Who is made to stumble, and I am not indignant?' (2 Corinthians 11:29).

Jeremiah is bound up with the God he serves, and the people he serves, and therefore his life and his ministry reflect both the nature of God, who overturns human standards of success, and the state of the people, lost in sin. So Jeremiah's failure in ministry is not due to his own incompetence; on the contrary, it is a sign of his closeness to God and to his people. True pastoral ministry which is built on a biblical model will always be ministry *in* God and *in* his people, but that is dangerous ministry because it will involve taking the risk of failing.

A Longer View

It's also worth remembering, of course, that the book of Jeremiah as we have it was not written by Jeremiah; it comes from a later editor, even though Jeremiah may well have been his own editor for the initial collection of his prophecy, and we know he was helped by

Baruch. But the book itself gives us a longer view, and that longer view shows us that Jeremiah's ministry was in some ways a real success. What he prophesied did come true – even the pagan Babylonians have to recognize that (40:2–3a). It may not have been an easy message to preach, but it was true, and God's truth will come to pass. Jeremiah is also, of course, just one book in the Bible. And the rest of the Bible shows us how his prophecies come true, and how his teaching helps to point the people of God, both in the exile and after the exile, back into the way of the true and living God. The longer view gives us a better understanding of the failures of his own lifetime; you cannot judge the effectiveness of ministry in the short term. A cousin of mine went to be vicar of a major parish in the north of England; he was a keen evangelist, and he felt that the people hated him because of his evangelistic zeal – he retired from there feeling that he had failed. Some years later a friend of mine went to be curate at that church at a time when it was experiencing enormous growth. 'Everything we are seeing happening here now,' he told me, 'we can trace back to Dick's ministry' – the ministry of the one who thought he had failed.

So one commentator sums up Jeremiah like this: 'It has often been remarked that Jeremiah's life was finally a failure. He was alone for most of his ministry. It seemed that no one gave any heed to his words. He was dragged off finally to live his last days in exile against his own will. He was a failure as the world judges human achievement. But a more balanced assessment of him would be that his very words of judgement saved Israel's faith from disintegration, and his words of hope finally helped his people to gain hope in God's future for them.'[6]

And I think there is even more to Jeremiah's importance than that, if we look at his experience of failure in the light of the whole Bible, in the light of Christ. Is it not central to the importance of Jeremiah that he points us forward to Jesus Christ? Jeremiah is one of God's suffering servants, and he prepares the way for the coming of *the* suffering servant, Jesus Christ. And Jesus' life and ministry ended in failure, surely? Is not the cross one of the greatest images of failure that there is? That is what it seemed like to many people at the time;

the cross is 'foolishness to the Greeks', says Paul, and it is certainly foolishness to many people today. Who wants to have anything to do with such a failure? I want to be successful, I do not want to be associated with a cross, a death, a failure.

But did Jesus Christ really fail? Was he not rather revealing the very nature of God when he hung there on the cross? Does he not show us that God does not offer a way of guaranteed success, but rather the way of the cross, the way of apparent failure, that the only way to life is via death? There is life, of course there is, glorious new life, Easter life, and Jeremiah points ahead to that also with his vision of hope, but he shows us that unless we grasp seriously the reality of failure, the reality of death, unless we are prepared to go through that failure ourselves, we shall never know the true reality of new life. He faced squarely the reality of his own failure, he brought it to God in all its starkness, and even had the temerity to consider the terrifying thought that God himself might have failed; as he did that he discovered the true nature of that failure, and indeed the true nature of God and of his hope that overcomes failure.

We shall have to face our own failure in pastoral ministry, we are members of a Church that has failed, we have to minister as pastors to those who feel they have failed. What shall we do with that failure? Shall we smooth it over with a sweet-smelling 'balm of Gilead' which does not really deal with the problem, or shall we face up to it squarely, shall we bring it openly to God, and shall we be prepared to ask that terrifying question 'Did Jesus fail?' Until we do that we shall not discover God's way through failure, we shall not understand our own failure, and we certainly shall not be able to offer anything that will really speak to the failure of others; we shall be paddling in the shallows instead of striking out into the depths. And that is what Jeremiah did; he did not just fail, he committed his cause to God (11:20), and struck out into the depths of failure and discovered what lay through it. And that is what Jesus did; he too 'committed his cause to the One who judges justly' (1 Peter 2:23 NEB), and struck out into the depths of failure so that we might discover what lies through it.

'What is God up to?'

'What is God up to?' — if we have never asked that question, then I suspect our own powers of pastoral observation need to be sharpened up, and our own prayer life needs to be deepened. If we need a model of someone whose powers of observation were acute, and whose prayer life touched great depths, then we need look no further than Jeremiah, who, as we have already seen, was never afraid to ask that question 'What is God up to?' But he was concerned not just to ask it in his own prayer and about his own experience, but to ask it in the context of current history, and to speak to God's people in such a way that they had to ask it for themselves, and face up to what the answer might be and might mean for them. Jeremiah is a true prophet, because like the prophets who came before him, he is a true expositor. He takes the Word of God — both the Word of the Law and the prophets of previous generations and the Word that was revealed directly to him — and he expounds it to his own generation, at the same time also expounding to them the meaning of current history. God is speaking in his Word, and so that can be expounded, but he is also at work, he is also speaking in current events, and so those need to be expounded too. God's pastoral work is not exclusively bound up in the pages of the Bible and in its exposition; he is not a library pastor but a living pastor, constantly at work *now*, and therefore true pastoral work is concerned with the exposition of the history of the people of God.

We tend to tie pastoral ministry up as ministry to individuals, and evangelicals in particular tend to reduce pastoral ministry to the ministry of biblical exposition. But, if we are to be true to the Bible itself, if we are to be true to Jeremiah as just one example of biblical pastoral ministry, we must liberate and broaden and enrich our understanding of the pastoral ministry we are called to, God's pastoral ministry in which he calls us, as he called Jeremiah, to share. If pastoral ministry is to have a genuinely prophetic edge to it, it must involve pastors working with the people of God to help them ask and answer the question 'What is God up to?'

God and Israel

Jeremiah's ministry was worked out against the background of two of the most significant events in Israel's history: the reformation which took place under King Josiah from *c*.622 BC, although the book of Jeremiah nowhere mentions this reformation directly, and the ongoing conflict with Babylon, which began with Judah's becoming a Babylonian vassal in 605/604 BC, and after various rebellions led to the two defeats and exiles of 597 BC and 587 BC. These two events are not simply significant historically, but also theologically, especially the second, which was a theological crisis unparalleled in Israel's history, because the fall of Jerusalem and the removal of such a large part of the population from the land of Israel seemed to destroy the covenant promises of God. Those promises had been underlined a century previously in Isaiah's prophecies to Hezekiah, that God would not abandon Jerusalem in the face of the Assyrian invasion (Isaiah 2:2–4; 14:32; 17:12–14; 28:14–19a; 29:5–8), and doubtless also by the Law book discovered in the Temple during the earlier part of Josiah's reign, which appears to have been a major stimulus to his reforms. If this book was either Deuteronomy or part of it, as seems very likely, there would again have been emphasized God's covenant promises to Jerusalem in view of the references in Deuteronomy to a chosen, central sanctuary (Deuteronomy 12:5–7,14,21; 14:23; 16:16). This covenant and its promises are the very basis of Israel's existence, they are certainly very important to Jeremiah, but God had to show the people of Judah something more than their simplistic reliance on the covenant had enabled them to see so far; he had to make them ask the question 'What is God up to?', and show them the answer.

First, he had to show them that *the covenant had been broken not from his side, but from theirs.* Jeremiah is called consistently to denounce the apostasy and idolatry which had flourished so openly under King Manasseh and his short-lived son, Amon (2 Kings 21), and which appears to have re-emerged in the reign of Josiah's son, Jehoiakim (607–597 BC). God abhors sacrifices made to false gods (7:30–34; 19:5–6; 32:34–35) and the immorality bound up with such apostasy

(5:1–9; 7:3–11; 23:10–14). And where true religion is abandoned, true justice is abandoned also, and the people had to face the reality of their sin in promoting injustice (21:12; 17:19ff.; 22:1ff.) Through Jeremiah, God consistently reminds his people of the demands of his covenant, and what results when that covenant is broken. There is no reason to doubt that Jeremiah himself emphasized consistently the demands of God's covenant, or to attribute covenant references to later 'Deuteronomic' editors.[7] The covenant expresses the heart of God's relationship with his people, and is naturally a central theme for Jeremiah, who sees with God's eyes that his people have broken that covenant (11:1–14).

Secondly, God had to show Israel that *the reforms of Josiah and the manner in which they had embraced them were not in themselves a sufficient response to his covenant demands.* We need not assume that Jeremiah was somehow lukewarm about those reforms. His approbation of Josiah in 22:15–16 suggests the opposite, but it is clear that he soon realized that those reforms in themselves were inadequate, and that God had more to say to his people. In a sense the reforms were dangerous, because they seem to have created a sense of complacency in the people: 'We have God's house and God's law, so we know we are safe.' This is the attitude that is attacked in Jeremiah's famous temple sermon in 7:1–29, which seems to belong to the time just after the death of Josiah. At that point in Israel's history it may be that the shallowness of the response to Josiah's reforms was being exposed by the obvious unwillingness of his son Jehoiakim to keep going down his father's road. Jeremiah is not opposed to the Temple and its cult, but he is opposed to any attitude which puts the Temple in the place which belongs to God himself. It is God alone who is the source of Israel's security, and not any institution, be it the ark (3:16), circumcision (4:4; 6:10; 9:25–26), the sacrificial system (6:20, 7:21–22; 14:11–12), the Torah (31:33–34), or the Temple itself (11:15, 26:1–15). Not all the people of Israel have practised simple idolatry, prevalent as that may have been, but a more subtle false religion has gripped them, a reliance on religious institutions that masks a deep disobedience (7:21–26). What is even worse is that the very people who should have led Israel away from such a false reliance on institutions, the priests and prophets, were themselves amongst the worst examples of this rebellion against God (5:30–31; 6:13–15; 14:13–15; 23:9–40; 28:1–17). There is a spiritual blindness amongst the very people called to show Israel the reality of their disobedience, but God, through Jeremiah, still makes his voice heard.

Thirdly, God shows his people that the exile is not just a matter of chance, nor simply a theological disaster, nor indeed that the gods of the Babylonians were stronger than himself, but that *the exile and the fall of Jerusalem were a judgement that sprang directly from their disobedience to him*. In New Testament words 'judgement begins with the family of God' (1 Peter 4:17). The great privileges of the people of God mean that they have a great responsibility. That is underlined by Jeremiah's concern for the people of the old northern kingdom of Israel, swept away by the Assyrians over a hundred years before. The merciful God calls the people of the north back to him (3:12), but at the same time he reminds Judah, the southern kingdom which was saved from the Assyrian takeover, that their privileged position makes them more guilty than the remnants of the northern kingdom (3:11). Because Judah has had the Temple and the prophets and the Law for so much longer than Israel, they are more liable to judgement, and Jeremiah's task is to urge God's people to face up to the reality of that judgement.

Judgement is, of course, a basic biblical theme; no theology that has any claim to be biblical can dispense with the judgement of God, and no one called to share in God's pastoral work can escape the responsibility of attempting to understand where God is at work in judgement. Jeremiah does not run away from that responsibility even though, as we have already seen, it costs him dearly. And the message of judgement is consistently found through the book of Jeremiah, in the poetic oracles (e.g. 10:17–22), the prose sermons (e.g. 11:11–12), the historical passages (e.g. 36:1–3), and the oracles against the nations (e.g. 48:13). The disasters of 597 BC and 587 BC are not meaningless catastrophes, but the righteous judgement of the covenant God.

But, fourthly, God has to show Israel that the *exile is not just an act of judgement, it is also an act of testing*, of cleansing. It is the turning point away from sin and judgement and failure to new life, it is a moment of transformation, of disclosure. It is not those who have been taken into exile who are sinful, they in fact are the good figs, as opposed to the bad figs left behind still trying to worm their way out of their predicament by dubious alliances and pointless plotting (24:1–10). Jeremiah is called to tell the people of Israel to hand themselves over to the Babylonians, and join those good figs (27:12–22), because, if the exile is a judgement, it is also an opportunity to discover God's new way, a time of testing and seeking (31:1–3).

And so, finally, God's message to Israel is one of *hope in and beyond the exile*. He has not stopped loving them, and he never will (31:3), and in Babylon they will find new hope. Even in the exile God will be with them; this is expressed in Jeremiah's remarkable letter to the exiles (29:1–23), which not only talks of a restoration to the land of Israel after seventy years (verses 10–14), but also calls on them to seek the peace and prosperity of Babylon in the present (verses 5–7). In Babylon itself they can and must live out the hope that God has for them. God can be closer to them, even in Babylon, than he has ever been before, and there will be a new covenant of intimacy between God and his people (31:31–34). It seems quite unnecessary to deny the authenticity of these verses as a genuine prophecy of Jeremiah: 'It is imperative that the investigator of a prophecy in Jeremiah, who believes that he has discovered the footsteps of a redactor, be very careful lest he limit the potential of the prophet himself to shade his own words and ideas.'[8] The day will come when the power of Babylon will be overthrown (chapters 50–51), and the editor's addition of the story of Jehoiachin's release, set in stark proximity to the gory details of the fall of Jerusalem in the historical appendix of chapter 52, highlights that message of hope, which is already beginning to be worked out in practice by the time the book reaches its final form; the good figs really are good figs and history proves it (24:6–7). Jeremiah stands firmly in the prophetic tradition in preaching and living out a message in which judgement and hope are inextricably woven together. God is at work in Israel to bring his hope to his people.

What is happening in Israel may seem like a catastrophe, national, personal, spiritual, and Jeremiah never minimizes the horror of it all, but in fact it makes theological sense because God is at work in all of it, and God, through Jeremiah and others, communicates the theological sense of it all to his people. God *is* a pastor to his people, seeking his sheep that are dispersed abroad, and his children who are in the midst of this naughty world, shepherding them away from what is false and into what is true, away from a trust in externals to a deeper relationship with himself, a bare trust in himself. One might even borrow Fowler's terms to see God in Jeremiah calling Israel from 'mythic-literal faith' right through to 'universalizing faith'.[9] In doing that God is always faithful to his covenant demand of righteousness and his covenant promise of love, and in that pastoral work he calls his servants to share.

Pastoring the People of God

Something of what God is doing and saying to Israel in the book of Jeremiah is expressed in a hymn of a great pastor of another age, John Newton:

> *These inward trials I employ,*
> *From self and pride to set thee free;*
> *And break thy schemes of earthly joy,*
> *That thou mayst seek thy all in me.*[10]

Newton was a pastor of such spiritual depth and self-understanding that he was able to apply God's Word to himself, to see that God was at work in his own experiences. But his hymn is very much directed towards himself as an individual, and is written for others to take and apply to their own individual experiences. Jeremiah, however, insists that we look at a broader canvas. God is at work not just in the pastor and the individuals, but in the whole history of the people of God. That is why Christians have a concern for church history, and do not just read Christian biographies, because God is at work in the history of the whole of his people and not just one or two, not just 'soul by soul and silently'. Reading biographies is the idiot's way of learning history, but it is also not a truly biblical way because the Bible insists that history is about the people of God and not just about individuals. So Jeremiah's task is to interpret what God is doing in his own day in the history of the people of Judah, and, indeed, the whole of Israel. And our pastoral task is not just to help this person or that person to understand what is going on in their own lives, but to speak to the whole people of God, or at least to that part of it which we are called to serve. We have to interpret for them what God is doing among them, and we are not left without help for that task, because we have the Scriptures, we have Jeremiah and his fellow prophets.

We have seen that one of the ways in which the Bible works pastorally is by illuminating our present situation for us. If we are ministering in a church which seems to be facing an exile situation, as in some ways I found myself doing in the parish of which I was incumbent in Bristol, then surely we need to go back to this book of Jeremiah and see how God's work there and then illuminates our circumstances here and now. Obviously we need to be aware of the differences in the situations, not least the fact that we live in the new covenant in Christ that Jeremiah only saw from afar, but we also need to be aware of the fact that we are dealing with the same God. And so we shall need to see in our situation how these themes from Jeremiah – God's covenant demands, the inadequacy of a shallow response to God, God's judgement, God's presence *in* the exile, God's promise of hope – speak to our situation, how they are being worked out in it, because God is at work in our situation, building a future and a hope for the people of God now, just as he was then.

God and the Individual

We have tried so far to examine how God is at work as a pastor in the situation of the book of Jeremiah. We have thought about God at work in Jeremiah himself, even in his failure, and God at work in his people Israel, even in their failure. But, of course, God has not just worked in one historical figure, Jeremiah, nor has he just worked in his people. He is alive and at work in people today, and he is alive and at work in the whole world, not just within the confines of the Church. After all, he created the world and loves it, and so he acts as a pastor in the world.

So we now need to take some of what I have been saying about God and Jeremiah, and move a little sideways from there to think about what this whole book has to say about God and the individual. We then shall need to take some of what I have been saying about God and Israel, and move forwards from there to think about the theme of God and the nations in Jeremiah.

Over the years it has been a basic axiom of interpretation of Jeremiah that he gives a new perspective on God's concern for individuals, an emphasis which he shares especially with his slightly younger contemporary, Ezekiel. Jeremiah 31:27–34 is, I suppose, the passage which more than any other has led interpreters to make this claim about Jeremiah; the same proverb about the sour grapes is taken up by Ezekiel (Ezekiel 18:1–32, cf. Ezekiel 33:1–20). One should perhaps beware of over-emphasizing the newness of this individual concern; it is undoubtedly present in Old Testament thinking before Jeremiah, particularly in the many accounts of godly individuals in the historical books and in the Wisdom literature. One should also beware of any suggestion that Jeremiah's concern is simply with individuals. As we have already clearly seen, he is called by God to minister to the whole nation of Israel, and to call the nation back to righteousness, not just as individuals, but in their relationships with one another (34:8–22).

But undoubtedly there is also a fresh understanding of the individual in relationship to God in Jeremiah. The book looks ahead to the exile and the *diaspora* which will result from it. Never again will the people of Israel live as a self-contained unit in their own land. Through Jeremiah, God prepares them for that *diaspora* by showing them that their future hope and security depend not just on the external Mosaic covenant, although as we have seen that was very important to Jeremiah and remains so, but also on a renewed covenant, under which God will change the hearts of men and women to bring them to a new knowledge of himself (31:31–34). The intimacy of Jeremiah's own relationship with God is an example of this new experience of God. This is an individual knowledge; as R. K. Harrison puts it: 'In practical terms this meant that the individual, when confronted with the new covenantal expression of divine love, would respond to it with a conscious act of will.'[11] But is Harrison not going too far when he also says: 'In looking for a time when people would be able to approach God on an individual basis rather than as members of an historically-covenanted group, Jeremiah was actually expecting the traditional covenant to be renewed in an even more glorious form,' and then directs our attention to 33:14–26?[12] Is not the point of chapter 33 precisely that the covenant is going to be *renewed*, and not completely overthrown and a new one set up with certain individuals (33:19–22)? And does not the very fact that God uses covenant terminology show that he is calling his people *together* to that new knowledge? Surely the idea of a covenant is irredeemably corporate, it speaks of unbreakable ties of unity between sovereign and people.

Jeremiah's vision of a new covenant looks forward not just to the people's return to exile, although in the first place it does do that, but also to the new covenant people who will live under the reign of the 'righteous branch sprouting from David's line' (33:15), in unity with him. And is it right to say that the people of this new covenant are not, as Harrison suggests, 'members of an historically-covenanted group'? We live under the new covenant sealed by the historical fact of the death of Christ, renewed for us week by week as we come to celebrate in a very material, historical, corporate meal the blood of the covenant that the righteous branch poured out for us.

So there is a new vision in Jeremiah for the day when people will have an intimate, personal knowledge of God and his law, but that does not mean that they will simply relate to him as individuals. In fact the whole context of chapter 31 is corporate – see, for example, verses 1–2, 10, 23–24 – and, of course, the promise of the new covenant is made to 'the house of Israel and the house of Judah' (v. 31). The other passage which speaks most clearly of the individual is

17:5–11, but again the context of that whole chapter is corporate; not only is Judah's sin corporate (v. 1), but their hope is corporate (verses 12–13a) – God is the hope of Israel and not just of one or two individuals.

Maybe the two aspects of the individual and the corporate are brought together in the idea of the remnant, a very familiar idea in Isaiah, but also present in Jeremiah, although he often uses the word 'remnant' without much theological significance, simply to describe the people left behind after the Babylonian invasion and deportation. But Jeremiah is also aware that God is creating his own remnant; that idea is, in fact, present in chapter 31 itself (31:7). God will restore his people after the exile, but it will not be all the people, it will be the good figs, the remnant (23:3). There is an element of God's call to return to him and then to his land being heard by individuals, but they come back to form together a remnant, a renewed covenant people (3:14). He calls them back one by one, two by two, to Zion, to the Temple, to his own presence, the centre of his people.

I think we are right to be suspicious of interpretations of Jeremiah which make out that he is the prophet of individual faith; they seem to me to be reading a modern Western individualism back into a text which in fact knows nothing of such a philosophy. We should not imagine that Jeremiah sat in his cistern thinking the same thoughts that Descartes had during his sojourn in the stove, or that Jeremiah the virtuoso prophet is something like Liszt the virtuoso pianist. In the cistern Jeremiah did not turn inwards to his own thoughts and his own existence, but rather felt the agony of being a prophet to a people who had rejected their covenant with God, he felt God's own agony over the fate of the nation; Jeremiah's own individual prayers show that he was no individualist. So God does have a pastoral concern for individuals, and we are right to share that concern, but Jeremiah shows us that such a concern must always be seen in the wider context of God's work in his people. A pastoral ministry built on biblical foundations, reflecting the work of Jeremiah's God, the God of the Bible, will have a right balance between the individual and the people of God.

God and the Nations

God's concern, however, goes far wider than just the affairs of Israel, and the book of Jeremiah, in the tradition of the Old Testament prophets, shows us that the God of Israel is the God of the Nations also. For Jeremiah, Yahweh is the only God, the Creator (10:11–13; 27:5), near at hand to his people and yet the Lord of all the universe (23:23–24), the Disposer of Israel (18:5–10) and of all the nations (25:15–38; 27:6–8). It is this monotheistic understanding which lies behind both the abhorrence of idolatry and the concern for the nations which are characteristic of the whole book. Some have tried to claim that the religion of Israel was essentially henotheistic, in other words it acknowledged Yahweh as the only God of Israel but recognized the existence of other gods for other nations. There is certainly no trace of such henotheism in Jeremiah; for him Yahweh is the one God of the whole world.

So Jeremiah is called to preach directly to the representatives of Israel's neighbours (27:1–11), and he sees that God is at work in the nations, even to the extent of calling Nebuchadnezzar his servant (27:6, cf. Cyrus in Isaiah 45:1). He sees also that God is the judge of the nations; chapters 46–51 contain a series of oracles of judgement against the nations, and raise the most serious critical questions concerning the book of Jeremiah, because they are obviously a distinct unit which probably originally circulated separately. In the Septuagint, the Greek translation of the Old Testament, these chapters appear in a different place in the book. However, neither the theme of judgement, nor the concern for the nations, is out of place in the wider context of the book, and collections of oracles against the nations are a typical feature of the prophetic books (Isaiah 13–23; Amos 1:2–2:16; Ezekiel 25–32). We should beware of ignoring these chapters just because they are obscure and not at first sight very appealing; they are just as much a part of the book of Jeremiah as any of the more familiar sections, and they are undergirded by important theological truths. They are certainly not just a xenophobic rant.

The theme of judgement is the most prominent in these chapters, but the judgement is not just an impersonal outworking of historical forces. *God is at work in the judgement.* Egypt's defeat comes on a 'day (that) belongs to the Lord, the Lord Almighty' (46:10), and the Philistines are destroyed by 'the sword of the Lord' (47:6). The nations do not just fail as part of the historical process, but for quite specific moral reasons (50:14). The sins of the nations are spelt out; they include pride (48:29), oppression (50:16) and idolatry (50:38).

The Lord of the nations, the Lord of so much power, is still the righteous Lord, and his moral demands are made on all. And, therefore, *his righteous work of judgement amongst the nations cannot be separated from his righteous work of judgement amongst his own people.* In one especially interesting passage in Jeremiah 48:11–17, there is a parallel drawn between God's work of judgement in Israel and in pagan Moab. Israel's history is bound up with the history of the nations, God is not treating them as quite separate groups, so there are parallels between what Israel is experiencing at the hand of the Babylonians and what Moab is experiencing from the same invading army – for both it is a judgement from the same God.

And indeed *Israel's hope is bound up with the history of the nations*, just as her judgement is (46:27–28). The last of these oracles, which is an oracle against Babylon, makes this link particularly clearly; the judgement that will fall on Babylon because of her sins will result in salvation for Israel (50:3–4). One aspect of the meaning of the fall of the Babylonians is that it is God's vengeance on them for the dishonour done to his worship by the destruction of Jerusalem (51:11).

At the same time, God's message to the nations is not exclusively one of judgement; we call these chapters oracles *against* the nations, but there is also *a message of hope for some of the nations*: Egypt – 46:26; Moab – 48:47; Ammon – 49:6; Edom – 49:11; Elam – 49:39. Is this just a later editor writing back into earlier oracles events after the destruction of the Babylonian empire, when some of the ancient nations of the Near East recovered something of their identity and independence, as Israel did? If it is, then surely the editor stands very close to Jeremiah's theology, which insists that God is at work in the world, in the good and the bad events, and which seeks to interpret the world, the nations in the light of God's truth. Does our ministry share that concern to understand the world, to discern how God is at work in the world? Does our contemporary understanding of the Church's pastoral task incorporate a willingness to see that the Church and the world are together under the hand of the one Disposer of all, to interpret the world to the Church just as we interpret the Scripture to the Church?

As we have already seen, the other passage of great importance for our understanding of how Jeremiah understands God's concern for the nations is Jeremiah's letter to the exiles in Babylon (29:1–32). The letter shows a concern for the peace and prosperity of that pagan city (29:7), and the exiles are to live out that concern in practice; the hope expressed and offered in the letter is also apparent in other oracles concerning the nations. Jeremiah sees a coming day when the nations will come to Jerusalem, united with Israel in worshipping the true God (3:17; 16:19–21). Just as there is judgement and hope for Israel, so there is judgement and hope for the nations.

Once again the book of Jeremiah testifies to the breadth of God's work in the world; he is no narrow-minded God, and those who are called to share in his work must share the breadth of his vision which encompasses the nations. There in itself is a challenge to our pastoral theology and vision.

God the Pastor

A pastoral study of the book of Jeremiah could simply concentrate on Jeremiah himself and the pastoral role he filled in Israel in his day. That would be an important picture, but it could be too narrow a vision. The Scriptures do not just present us with models of working to be imitated by us. In fact, as we have already pointed out, to search the Bible for such models can be dangerous, because we live at such a distance from the people we meet within its pages. The models cannot be neatly transported across thousands of years to the last days of the twentieth century; if we attempt to do so, we shall probably be acting in a quite inappropriate manner. But that is not to say that the Bible has nothing to say to us, no authority to which we must submit. We have to look beyond the models to the principles underlying them, the theology and experience of God which inspires them, and allow that understanding to inform our own working, to mould appropriate models for us to use in our pastoral care today. Jeremiah is a rich source of such principles, a major contributor to Christian theology, an important guide for Christian experience, because he directs our attention away from himself to God and his pastoral work, in Jeremiah, in Israel and in the nations. This work of God is the only source of Jeremiah's ministry. To meditate on the nature and the work of the God we meet in the pages of Jeremiah will, I believe, illuminate the Church's pastoral calling in every age, and enrich our understanding of our pastoral task today.

Notes

1. Anderson, R. S. (Ed.), *Theological Foundations for Ministry*, Edinburgh, T. & T. Clark, 1979
2. Holladay, W. L., *Jeremiah*, Vol. 2, Minneapolis, Fortress, 1989
3. cf. Wharton, J. A., in Shelp, E. E. and Sunderland, R., (Eds), *A Biblical Basis for Ministry*, Philadelphia, Westminster, 1981, pp. 17–71
4. Zimmerli, W., *The Fruit of the Tribulation of the Prophet*, ET in Perdue, L. G., and Kovacs, B. W. (Eds), *A Prophet to the Nations*, Winona Lake, Eisenbrauns, 1984, p. 361
5. Newbigin, Lesslie, *Foolishness to the Greeks*, London, SPCK, 1986
6. Thompson, J. A., *The Book of Jeremiah*, Grand Rapids, NICOT, Eerdmans, 1980, p. 106
7. cf. Untermann, J., *From Repentance to Redemption*, Sheffield, JSOT Press, 1987
8. ibid., p. 178
9. Fowler, J. W., *Stages of Faith*, San Francisco, Harper & Row, 1981
10. *Olney Hymns*, Book III, No. 36
11. Harrison, R. K., *Jeremiah and Lamentations*, London, Tyndale Press, 1973, p.42
12. ibid., p. 41

Part Four

EVANGELICAL PASTORAL WRITERS AND THE BIBLE

Introduction

As we have already pointed out, evangelicals customarily proclaim 'the final authority of Scripture in all matters of faith and conduct' as a basic axiom of Christian faith. It is, of course, one thing to proclaim that authority, and quite another to work it out in thinking and practice. A careful study of the Bible leads Christians to affirm that, in God's plan, sexual intercourse belongs inside marriage. How that authoritative position affects the way in which a Christian pastor ministers to an already cohabiting couple who ask to be married in his church is much more difficult to work out, as any pastor will affirm. If evangelicals are to be true to their heritage and their stated doctrinal position, they need to be carefully and thoroughly biblical, not just in their opinions but in their actions.

The aim of the final part of this book is to examine how four evangelical writers on pastoral work live up to their stated aim to be biblical. How true are they to their heritage? The four writers are Jay Adams and his 'Theology of Christian Counselling' *More than Redemption*,[1] Lawrence Crabb, author of *Understanding People*,[2] Roger Hurding and his *Roots and Shoots*,[3] and Derek Tidball, whose 'Introduction to Pastoral Theology' is called *Skilful Shepherds*.[4]

My aim here is not to give a complete survey of the writings of these authors; that would be a major task, especially in the case of Adams and Crabb, who are both prolific writers in this area. Others are much better situated that I am to make such an assessment of a complete career in pastoral writing. What I want to do is, noting the popularity of these authors, to look at four books written by them, which happen to be amongst the most likely to appear on the library shelf of anyone engaged in and concerned to think carefully about Christian pastoral ministry.

It should be mentioned that there is a measure of interaction between these four books and authors; both Hurding and Tidball comment at some length on Adams, and Hurding also assesses Crabb. Crabb makes little direct reference to Adams, but he is undoubtedly writing for people who have read Adams.

JAY ADAMS' *MORE THAN REDEMPTION*

The Bible as Textbook

Jay Adams is an American pastor in the Reformed tradition. In the course of his pastoral ministry in the late fifties and early sixties he attempted to counsel people using various psychotherapeutic methodologies, Freudian, Rogerian, etc. Increasingly he found such methodologies unsatisfactory. In the light of the joint challenge of having to prepare courses in pastoral counselling at Westminster Theological Seminary and of spending several months observing the work of the 'anti-psychiatrist' O. H. Mowrer, Adams began to develop a new system which he called 'Nouthetic Counselling'.[5] This title is derived from the Greek word *noutheteo*, 'the principal and the fullest biblical word for counselling'.[6]

Adams sets out Nouthetic Counselling's basic principles as, firstly, the supreme authority of the Bible – 'The Bible is [the Christian's] counselling textbook'.[7] Secondly, all nonorganic problems have a moral character – 'All nonorganically caused problems are considered to be hamartiagenic [sin-caused].'[8] Thirdly, for those who believe in Christ (although not for others), all problems can be solved through his saving power and by his Holy Spirit.[9]

This leads to a counselling system in which the basic aim is to discover the sin which has created the problem for the counsellee, confront that sin, and then lead the counsellee to an experience of forgiveness and the 'dehabituation' of the relevant sinful habit and 'rehabituation' in biblical behaviour patterns. *More than Redemption* is not a book of case studies, but Adams does make some suggestions of how this approach works out in practice.

You must make it perfectly clear to the counsellee that suffering can never be handled properly (or turned into the blessing God intends it to be for his children) until rebellion disappears. Hot-tempered rebellion so clouds one's perception of a situation that he sees nothing but the negative aspects of it. Pain and suffering for every Christian can *always* be turned to a blessing when *used* (rather than resisted or complained about) as God's Word directs. [10]

Adams' work has been both greatly admired and severely criticized, perhaps for the same reasons. His style is highly opinionated and sweeping, making it easy for the reader to be taken along with him in his argument; for the evangelical reader that is, perhaps, accentuated by Adams' liberal use of biblical quotations. This sweeping style, however, is also calculated to anger his readers. It could even be described as an inherently unpastoral style, because Adams appears not to listen to the wisdom of others, but rather to have an unbounded confidence in his own thinking, his own interpretation of Scripture. Adams also wins friends and makes enemies by his readiness to take a stand against what appears to many to be the surrender of American pastoral care to the psychotherapeutic professionals. So often they seem to Adams to operate with entirely humanistic, if not anti-Christian, presuppositions. Again one can see that this stand is appealing to many who long for an escape from an American preoccupation with 'therapy'. British readers, who are particularly suspicious of this example of modern American culture, may feel themselves allies of Adams here.

Adams is a Christian representative of the 'anti-psychiatry' school, which is also associated with the names of Szasz, Laing and Adams's own teacher, Mowrer, and especially with Ken Kesey's novel and film *One Flew over the Cuckoo's Nest*.[11] This reaction of the anti-psychiatrists is, in many ways, a healthy one, but, like many reactions, it tends to be one-sided and ill-balanced. The anti-psychiatrists rightly rebel against the tyranny of psychiatry, which is so often seen as the solution to any problem. In the process, however, they seem to go too far in the direction of rejecting the whole idea of mental illness. Any Christian pastor, however, will be suspicious of this rejection of mental illness. Pastors are all too familiar with the situation of a person in distress who knocks at the door without any warning. To class all such people as mentally ill and in need of psychotherapeutic treatment is dangerous; it may well miss the whole point of their problem. But it is equally true that some of these people will indeed be mentally ill, and the Christian pastor's task is to be aware of a situation she cannot deal with, and gently pass the person on to someone else more skilled in that area.

Much criticism of Adams is provoked by his own lack of balance, which is strikingly similar to that of the anti-psychiatrists. He seems to dismiss his opponents sweepingly, regularly alluding to them without giving references to their works (although he is an enthusiastic cross-referencer of his own material). It is hardly surprising that some of his critics become decidedly angry when he writes like this: 'Does the reader think for one moment that Skinner or Harris or Mowrer has solved his own problems? Did Freud? Study his biography. His addiction to cocaine reveals something of his failure to do so.'[12] Not only are there no references here, but what he says about Freud, at least, is some way from the rather complex truth of Freud's experimentation with cocaine.[13]

The apparently blind arrogance of Adams can be equally infuriating. Although, at times, he does acknowledge a debt to Mowrer, he frequently affirms that 'Nouthetic methodology is not borrowed from other systems'.[14] What is more, because Nouthetic counsellors do not believe that true counselling can be offered to the unregenerate, Adams claims that 'Nouthetic counsellors look on all other counselling as shallow and inadequate.'[15] Adams does not give references to the writings of any other Nouthetic counsellors. It is clear, however, that he is claiming much for his own system. It is not just different, or offered as a possible improvement, or an important corrective; it is inherently superior to all other systems of counselling. This dismissal of all other counselling could be likened to the enthusiast for alternative medicine who rejects traditional medicine completely. Maybe there is a need to challenge some of the assumptions of traditional medicine, but to reject it completely is to become dangerously unbalanced.

Some critics seem, hardly surprisingly, to be as impatient of Adams as he would perhaps be of them. His (deliberately?) antagonistic style has riled them into an annoyed response. This leads to some inaccurate and undeserved criticism of his position. H. Clinebell, for instance, accuses Adams, in a very brief critique, of preventing people from discovering the Bible as the living Word.[16] But is it precisely because Adams believes that the Bible is living, performative, that he uses it in the way he does — 'It is the Word ministered to counsellees that brings about spiritual change (2 Timothy 3:15–17) and growth (1 Peter 2:2)'[17] and 'The Spirit works through His Word; that is how He works.'[18] S. Pattison offers a somewhat lengthier and more helpful critique of Adams, but he also fails to tackle Adams on his own ground. Pattison's own understanding of Scripture is not an evangelical one. He describes his own position over against an evangelical understanding as follows: 'The presence of the living Lord in Church and world relativizes the importance of Scripture — Scripture itself bears witness to this.'[19] Pattison makes some important points, but in the end his theological position prevents his tackling Adams on his own ground, and will make his criticisms appear unconvincing to Adams' evangelical followers.

More than Redemption claims to be a theology of Christian counselling. It is an attempt to relate biblical doctrine to the world of counselling and, in the process, provide a justification for Adams' system of Nouthetic Counselling. If Adams is to be criticized in a way which will be effective in the evangelical constituency, we must examine his understanding of the Bible and the doctrine it teaches. It is precisely there that I believe Adams to be vulnerable. He displays a large biblical knowledge, but he frequently fails to see the deeper implications of the very biblical doctrines he is so happy to press into the service of Nouthetic Counselling. Let us examine some of those areas of doctrine.

Creation

Does Adams believe in Creation in the sense that the biblical writers do? Does he believe that this world, and the human beings who live in it, are created by God? Does he believe that they all reflect something of him as their Creator? Obviously, at one level, Adams firmly believes in Creation, and has much to say about it. His conclusions are straightforward and uncontroversial: 'Adam ... was created to live in an exciting, productive, God-honouring manner that would bring joy and satisfaction to him.'[20] But he also seems to believe that the Fall has obliterated every trace of God's image in unregenerate men and women. 'Accompanying the ruin of the image of God was the ruin of human capacity for true knowledge, righteousness and holiness.'[21] 'Ruin' seems to be a key word in Adams' statement of the Fall. As a result, the way in which he develops his work implies that God is no longer at work in creation because his image in creation has been totally 'ruined' – nothing of God can be found in human history. Adams seems to find no place for general revelation, for common grace; truth can be found only in the special revelation of the Scriptures. This attitude appears to be at odds with many in Adams' own Reformed tradition. Calvin, for instance, is very clear that sinful, unconverted human beings are not outside the righteous action of God in this world: 'Therefore, whatever men or Satan himself devise, God holds the helm, and makes all their efforts contribute to the execution of his judgements.'[22]

Adams' understanding of creation also leads him into damaging inconsistencies. He appears inconsistent in his use of biblical texts about it. He makes much use of Genesis 1–3 and some parts of the Wisdom tradition when he refers to the Old Testament. The early chapters of Genesis show us the essential nature of human beings, created by God but totally flawed by original sin. The book of Proverbs sets out the pattern of Nouthetic Counselling, the giving of godly advice to turn people away from sin and into righteousness. However, he fails to see the implications of other parts of the Old Testament. Why, for instance, does he make so little of the historical books, or of the prophets with their vision of God at work even in the wider, pagan world (e.g. Isaiah 45, Jeremiah 29)? Why does he ignore Jesus' clear statement that God is profoundly concerned for and involved in the lives of the 'unrighteous' just as he is for the 'righteous' (Matthew 5:45)?

He is inconsistent in that he has to admit that truth may be discovered in Creation and history, but claims that only the Bible tells us all the truth about human nature. He retains the idea of counselling, which is, as Pattison points out, not biblical but modern, and he certainly uses modern methods of communication to promote Nouthetic Counselling, so we have to presume that he believes that good ideas can develop across history. But in what he writes he appears not to believe that history can tell us anything true about human beings. Why, he asks, do we use the Bible as a textbook in counselling but not in other areas? 'The Bible was not intended to be a textbook for engineering, medicine, etc., but it *was* intended to be the textbook for helping people come to love God and their neighbours.'[23] We shall have more to say about Adams' use of the Bible later.

He is inconsistent also in acknowledging a debt to Mowrer, but steadfastly refusing to say that he is a disciple of Mowrer. Adams seems to possess no understanding of his own thought being part of an ongoing history of thought about counselling, and therefore of God's ongoing work of creation. He does not see that he is within a tradition himself, although he happily criticizes other traditions of psychology.

There is, in fact, a thoroughgoing and unbiblical dualism in Adams' thinking which belies the doctrine of Creation which he professes. He is dualistic in believing that the Creation is either in Satan's hands or God's: 'The Bible's position is that all counsel that is not revelational [biblical] or based upon God's revelation, is Satanic.'[24] Here he seems to be applying the 'two kingdoms' theology of Van Til to counselling theory.

He is dualistic, as we have seen, in believing that although history teaches the truth about some things, only the Bible does so about human nature. He is dualistic in his understanding of human nature: it is material and spiritual, body and heart,[25] when the biblical picture as a whole, Old Testament and New Testament, would seem to see human beings as quite complex unities. He needs such an anthropology to justify his counselling system, which appears to see no place for emotions. Counselling is all to do with behaviour patterns, for which we are morally responsible. Emotions, it seems, are no more than the consequences of right or wrong behaviour patterns. 'He would appear to have no understanding of the complex interactions of genetic predispositions and life events.'[26]

He is dualistic in his understanding of the regenerate and the unregenerate. One cannot offer true counselling to non-believers, because they are incapable of change; they can only be given 'pre-counselling', i.e. evangelism of a fairly direct kind. But is God not also concerned for the unregenerate? Does he not want their situation to change in this world? If he did not, then none of them would ever become regenerate. Adams writes as follows: 'Surely a business man can't be conducting his business affairs according to the principles of Colossians 3 *before* he comes to know Christ. Well, then, why not tell him about the need to be working for Christ rather than for an ungrateful employer? A new convert's family relationships can't be Christian before he is, so why not ask about the family right away?'[27] Isn't Adams' 'surely' a little desperate? Surely, in fact, a business man may well be following the highest principles of business ethics which have been built up through the influence of countless Christians in business over the years, even though he himself does not (yet!) acknowledge Christ? May not a family be 'sanctified' by one Christian member (1 Corinthians 7:14), even though others do not share her faith? God does not give over everything in the world to chaos; instead he restrains the power of sin in his love and care for his own Creation, even though it is fallen and rebellious (2 Thessalonians 2:6).

Adams is also dualistic in his understanding of the Church and the world. Although he attacks independency and Darbyism, his theology seems to be leading him in a similar direction, because he seems to believe that the Church has nothing to learn from the world – 'There should never be a need for a member of Christ's Church to turn to a social worker,'[28] but may not God have given to that social worker particular skills that a particular Christian needs? And surely the Bible offers us at least one example of a member of God's people, a prophet no less, who had a great deal to learn from pagans, and that is Jonah. An essential part of the message of Jonah is that the pagan sailors and Ninevites are more righteous than Jonah, who is not only a member of God's people but also a prophet. The sailors believe that God is with them on the boat, while Jonah believes that he can run away from God. The Ninevites repent and obey when they hear God's message. Jonah not only disobeys God's first call to go and preach to them, he also grumbles and complains about God's kindness in not destroying them. The book of Jonah seems to be there in our Bibles to remind us not to draw too sharp a dividing line between God's people, the Church, and the world around us. God is at work in the wider world, and therefore the Church can learn from it.

Adams may proclaim belief in Creation, but the manner in which he develops his work is in fact dualistic: the world is generally bad, and only people who are converted to Christ are good. Dualism, however, can claim to be no better than sub-Christian, and sub-biblical. The first pages of our Bibles show us not only that all the world is God's Creation (Genesis 1), but also that, even after the Fall, God is still concerned for what he has created (Genesis 4). In the New Testament Paul attacks those who write off the world as bad (1 Timothy 4:3–5). We do well to hear those warnings, and not to fall into the same trap as some did in Paul's day.

Sin

At first sight it might seem ridiculous to ask whether Adams really believes in sin and the Fall. After all, his whole system is based on the understanding that all nonorganic human problems are the result of human sin, including the sin of the counsellee. He does not claim that problems and suffering are visited on individuals in direct proportion to their own sin,[29] but problems are still related to the sin of the individual concerned – 'Nonorganic causes of suffering and pain ... indicate that there is something wrong in the attitudes or the behaviour of the one who suffers.'[30]

But, one must ask, is the biblical picture of the effects of the Fall and of original sin merely one in which the moral understanding of individuals has been overturned? The picture of Romans 8:18–23 shows us that the Fall has affected every relationship within the universe. The whole of the created order is groaning in its pain and expectation. Contemporary concern for the environment seems here to be in tune with Paul's analysis of a broken world, indeed a broken universe. Paul has to struggle for words in this remarkable passage, which shows that much more has been affected by sin than individual morals; humanity's entire make-up and environment have been damaged. People are affected and damaged by much more than simply their own wrong behaviour. They are often caught up quite unwillingly in a whole complex of wrong relationships created by the sin of others. Family therapy, with its analysis of the systems of relationships in which people grow up, confirms this truth. There is also such a thing as structural sin. Injustice can damage a whole community. The minister working in a broken-down 1950s housing estate on the edge of a European city once reliant on heavy industry, and the small Pentecostal church struggling to build up its life in the slums of a Brazilian provincial capital, do not need to be convinced of the reality of structural sin. The pastor's task in such a community is not merely to confront individuals with their wrong behaviour patterns, although he will be concerned to do this, but also to support them in their suffering, and to understand what steps need to be taken to overcome the sinful structures which oppress them. The biblical image of the Christian leader as 'pastor' or 'minister' is not in the first place a confrontational picture. 'Pastors' are shepherds, whose first duty is to care for their flock, supporting them and carrying their burdens. 'Ministers' are servants, whose first task is to make others' needs their priority.

This somewhat shallow understanding of sin appears to affect Adams' understanding of guilt also. He says that even when an individual does not live according to biblical standards, that person's sense of guilt must not be rejected as false; it is still true for that person. He quotes Romans 14:23,[31] although without drawing out the context of that chapter, in which Paul is dealing with a specific question relating to whether Christians should eat meat offered to idols or not, and without seeing that verse in the light of, for example, Romans 1:18–32. If Romans 14 cannot be seen as enunciating general principles, Romans 1 certainly can. But Adams does not appear to see the implications of what Paul is saying in Romans 1. Part of Paul's argument there is that the Fall has perverted people's consciences. Their sense of guilt can be simply misplaced. One of the aims of the Christian counsellor is not simply to accept every guilt feeling in a counsellee at face value. We have to attempt to educate that person's conscience so that it is truly in line with God. A shallow understanding of sin and the Fall leads to a shallow understanding of guilt too. That could be very dangerous in the whole of Christian life, in helping people to pray and witness, as well as in counselling.

Incarnation

Adams makes the important point that the Incarnation presents us with a picture of human normality, and that this gives an authoritative basis to Christian counselling – 'Christ, not sociological polls, provides the norms for human living'.[32] This is vital for Christian counsellors. We do not have to invent our own understanding of what it is to be normal; God has given it to us in the life of Jesus Christ.

But again we find Adams apparently unable to draw out the implications of God's taking humanity on himself, the fact that he 'lifts our humanity to the heights of his throne'. This must radically affect the way in which we, as Christians, treat our fellow human beings. None of us measures up to God's picture of humanity; we always have to remember that we all fall short of God's best. But the humanity of every individual has nevertheless been enhanced and glorified by God's own coming into the world. God has not just cast us aside as worthless sinners, but taken our human nature on and into himself. Therefore we can never treat people as simply sinners; they may be ruins, in one sense, but there is glory among the ruins. All of us involved in any kind of pastoral work need to remember that, and hold together that tension, just as Jesus did when he talked to the Samaritan woman, and invited himself to dinner at Zacchaeus' house.

Adams, however, seems again to be inconsistent here. Having said that Christ provides the norms for human being, he seems to move back to a pre-Christian position by saying that 'Counsellors are lawmen'.[33] Law, of course, has its proper place in Christian theology and ethics, but it derives its proper place only from Christ. In the light of Christ and his coming we see that people need not merely the condemnation of law, but also the respect and love that Jesus himself showed time and time again. Surely as Christians we must say that 'Counsellors are Christ-men and -women'.

The Cross

As Adams points out, the cross is vital for Christian counselling, because it is the cross which gives meaning to human suffering.[34] But again it seems that Adams is unable or unwilling to follow through all the deep implications of the cross. He states clearly the place of the cross as the event which makes sense of suffering, but elsewhere forgets this, and seems to see the cross as simply a solution to our human problem. He jumps swiftly from the mystery of the cross to the triumph of the resurrection without reflecting on the fact that one can only arrive at the resurrection if one has taken up the cross. The cross is, of course, a solution, God's ultimate solution to humanity's ultimate problem, but it is no simple solution.

The theology of the cross recognizes the tensions in Christian existence, exposing them for what they really are and allowing us a realistic sense of perspective into our situation. The cross and resurrection demonstrate and illuminate the genuine tension between the 'here and now' and 'there and then' in the life of the individual believer and the church, and prohibit the elimination of this tension if an authentically *Christian* understanding is to result'.[35]

But Adams seems to believe that the Christian life should not have such tensions. He decries perfectionism, but in practice seems to believe in it. He rightly emphasizes that the eschatological perspective of Christianity gives us hope, the vital need of so many people.[36] However, he seems to forget that the same eschatological perspective reminds us that the solution of some problems, the wiping away of every tear, must remain in the future. And yet that does not leave us in despair in the present, because the cross gives meaning to our present situation, not just a way out of it. Jesus died and rose again in this world, and our suffering in this world can be a reflection of his cross. If I go to visit a member of our college community in hospital after a serious operation, I do not go to ensure that she has a right attitude to her suffering. My aim is not to check that her attitude is not sinful, and, if it is, tell her that she needs to be forgiven and can be through the cross. I go to play my part in assuring her that her suffering is not pointless, it does not place her outside God's care and purpose. I do that by showing her something of that care in gentle listening, and by acknowledging something of that suffering through my open willingness to face it by visiting the hospital. My position as a leader and representative of the wider Christian community adds another element to that process of bringing together her suffering and Jesus's cross, because I am the one who has been officially commissioned to speak, in some way, in the name of Jesus. As a minister, a Christian pastor, my own life has to be marked by the cross, the mark of Jesus.

The Church

One of the strengths of Adams' position is the importance he attaches to the Church.[37] He refuses to leave counselling in the hands of a few experts, and believes that every Christian can and should have a counselling role towards his or her fellow believers. In fact, Adams is quite clear that true counselling can only be done in the Church. Pastors have a particular responsibility as counsellors, because counselling is part of the ministry of the Word.[38]

Much of this is a very healthy redress of attitudes which seem to have been seduced by the expertise of psychotherapy. Here Adams is in line with the emphasis of contemporary pastoral theology, which wants to rescue pastoral care from its image of 'dealing with crises' through some kind of 'therapy'. Pastoral care which is genuinely Christian is neither negative, concerned only with dealing with problems, nor individualistic, directed only towards the person who presents a problem. Adams' emphasis on the Church is certainly in line with the biblical picture of the Body of Christ; it is incidentally also in line with the anti-psychiatrists' emphasis on the importance of the 'healing community', rather than leaving 'healing' solely in the hands of medical experts. People do not, indeed cannot, recover mental health on their own, because a central aspect of good mental health is the ability to construct good relationships.

But how far does Adams go into the biblical picture of the Church? His idealistic picture of the Church seems to forget that the people of God were very much a mixed multitude when they left Egypt. The mixture certainly did not become much purer through Old Testament history. Not only are Canaanite Rahab and Moabite Ruth welcomed in, as the New Testament genealogies pointedly remind us, but the history writers and prophets keep demonstrating to us that Israel gets things very wrong indeed. The New Testament also shows us that the Church is composed of a great mixture of people, problem people at different levels of growth and with different levels of experience as Christians. Jesus' own apostles, handpicked for the task, lack understanding of his ministry, and make endless practical mistakes. The Pauline churches cause their founder great pain, along with much joy. The seven churches of Revelation may be pictured as stars in God's right hand, but their brightness is far from unsullied. One must not lose the ideal picture of the Church, but Adams seems to think that the ideal is fairly easy to attain; the Bible would appear to suggest otherwise.

Conversion

Adams has a strong doctrine of conversion: no one is naturally a Christian, naturally regenerate, all need to be converted. In that he is a thoroughgoing evangelical, and evangelicals would accept that this is the biblical pattern. But does Adams go beyond the biblical pattern? He seems to believe not just that conversion and regeneration are necessary, but that they are invariably instantaneous and easily observable. This belief underlines his conviction that true counselling can be offered only to Christians. For non-Christians only 'pre-counselling' is appropriate – the problem can only really be dealt with when the person has been converted.[39]

The biblical pattern of conversion, however, seems to be rather more complex than Adams allows. For Paul and the Philippian gaoler conversion may have been an instantaneous experience, but was it for the apostles, for Peter, say, or Thomas? And what about Timothy or the household of Stephanas? Experience of ordinary evangelical church life suggests that the biblical picture is truer than the one which Adams appears to accept. Some people are converted instantaneously, but for others the period of transition may be quite lengthy. Still others will grow up as Christians and never be able to pinpoint one moment of conversion. This is the range of people pastors are called to counsel, people who are all on the way. While the experienced counsellor will be spiritually discerning, she or he cannot judge exactly who is regenerate and who is not; that judgement is God's, and not the counsellor's. To believe in the universal need for conversion is not the same as to believe that all conversions must follow a certain set pattern or will be easily observable.

The Bible

Every page of Adams' work breathes his conviction that Nouthetic Counselling is *the* biblical system of counselling, but that claim must, I think, be challenged, and has been done so with some frequency.[40] In the first place, he seems to be very selective in his use of the

Scriptures; the choice of the word *noutheteo* is, in itself, an example of that selectivity.

It should be pointed out that the word *noutheteo* in fact occurs only nine times in the New Testament; the noun *nouthesia* is found three more times. All of these occurrences are in the Pauline writings, apart from Acts 20:31, where Luke places it on the lips of Paul. It is not a word found in the gospels, the Johannine writings or the other epistles. The NRSV is typical of modern translations in rendering it 'warn' or 'instruction' or 'admonition'. Most of the uses of it appear to refer to corporate contexts of Christian teaching or proclamation. In Titus 3:10 Paul uses it to describe the 'admonition' given to a person who causes divisions, but presumably this refers to an admonition given by the church or someone who represents the whole body of the Church. One could not easily draw a parallel with modern counselling from these uses.

The word 'group' is also very rarely used in the Greek Old Testament (or Septuagint): *noutheteo* is found eight times in Job, but the only other occurrence of it is in 1 Samuel 3:13. NRSV, relying, of course, on the Hebrew text, follows AV (KJV) in translating the 1 Samuel reference as 'restrain'. As the Hebrew and Greek texts of Job vary considerably, it is difficult to draw any conclusions from English versions based on the Hebrew. Brenton's translation of the Septuagint translates variously as 'instruct', 'reprove', 'rebuke' and 'admonish'. The con-text here is generally Job's need to hear a message of instruction from others or from God. It is therefore used of an individual's receiving instruction. *Nouthesia* only appears in the Apocrypha, where there are three other uses of *noutheteo*, all in the book of Wisdom.

Why does Adams not use another, and far more frequently found, NT word – *parakaleo*? One is tempted to answer that the idea of *parakeleo* or *paraklesis*, which is often translated as 'calling alongside to help', does not fit with Adams' presupposed moral model of counselling, which demands an element of admonition or confrontation. In fact there is a variety of both Hebrew and NT Greek words which could properly be investigated in the process of building a truly biblical approach to counselling, but Adams seems unable to get beyond *noutheteo*.

As we have already seen, Adams is also selective in the biblical books he investigates and uses in his counselling system. He uses Genesis 1–3 and Proverbs a great deal, but, in spite of mentioning Job from time to time, he fails to get to grips with the depths of that book. Can a system claim to be biblical when it is built on such a limited selection of biblical ideas and books? Does 'biblical' simply mean quoting the Bible, or using one particular group of stories or one strand of its thinking? The Bible is indeed given to us as a library of different books, written over a vast period of time, each one of which needs to be considered seriously in its own right, but it is also given to us as a canon, a whole package which we must consider as a whole. We have to listen to the debate between the different elements going on within its covers, as well as to the message of the individual voices.

Adams is selective also in his methods of Bible study, showing a concern mainly for word studies. Some of these become more and more bizarre, as he reads more and more meanings out of particular words. *More than Redemption* contains a series of such word studies, the oddest of which, perhaps, is one on baptism.[41] The most basic lesson of hermeneutics is that words do not necessarily mean their etymology, but etymological speculation dominates Adams' word studies. 'It would be impossible to explain all words as if the etymology was the guide to their semantics without making chaos of language.'[42]

This apparent concern to draw meanings out of words in order to justify a particular system has been taken to its ultimate lengths in Adams' own translation of the New Testament – *The Christian Counsellor's New Testament*, a translation apparently done from the point of view of the nouthetic counsellor. Life certainly becomes a lot easier if one can use a Bible translated from one's own point of view! This seems to be the tactic adopted by sub-Christian sects such as the Jehovah's Witnesses and Christian Scientists. 'The pigeonholes are set up; Bible verses and terms are then tucked into them', is Adams' description of the methodology of 'Christian Freudians',[43] but he seems to do exactly the same, squeezing the Bible into his own pigeon-holes, marked 'confrontation', 'individual moral responsibility', 'sin and forgiveness' and so on, perhaps using rather more Bible verses.

In *More than Redemption* Adams constantly pleads for close co-operation between biblical theology and the world of counselling; the two must be held together if counselling is to be truly Christian. But he himself shows virtually no sign of interaction with biblical theologians. In his word studies he seems to interact rather more with the Oxford English Dictionary. This is not only inconsistent with his stated beliefs about the Bible, but also about the Church. As we have seen, he emphasizes the importance of the Church, but he seems to find no role for his fellow Christians in the task of under-standing the Bible correctly. Biblical theologians are a gift to the Church, they are not best ignored in favour of a dictionary.

Adams also seems to believe that the Bible is easy to interpret. He appears to have no difficulty in discovering what the Bible has to say on any particular subject; there is little hard work to be done. A doctrine much valued by evangelicals is the perspicuity of Scripture, the belief that what we need to know for our salvation can be clearly grasped in Scripture by quite simple minds – Scripture is trans-parent. But evangelicals also want to affirm that the Bible is both the word of human beings who lived in a distant age and a foreign culture, and the Word of God, whose thoughts are far above our thoughts. Precisely because it is the Word of *God* the Bible is not always easy for us human beings, with our limited minds, to under-stand. There is hard grammatical, historical, critical, theological, prayerfully contemplative work to be done if we are to plumb the depths of Scripture.

And let us beware of following Adams in saying that the Bible is a textbook of human nature. It is not meant to be the *textbook* of anything; if God had intended it to be a textbook, surely he would have arranged its contents rather differently. The Bible is all true, but it certainly does not contain every truth. What it offers us is not easy-to-turn-up information, but a pattern within which we can understand ourselves and our world, our past and our future; it enables us to see all this not just from our point of view, but from God's point of view. It does so not by giving us systematic informa-tion like an encyclopaedia or textbook, but by recounting history, telling stories, listening to oracles, sharing spiritual struggles, wrestling with doctrine and seeing visions of glory. We have to allow our minds to get inside the different methods of communication that the Bible uses if we are to understand its message; we cannot simply read all of that message off the page at first sight.

Adams' biblical concern is, in itself, admirable; he opens doors which enable new light to be shed in an area which many Christians have abandoned. His willingness to understand counselling in a biblical light is in itself a challenge to all Christians involved in pastoral care, not to abandon their commitment to biblical authority in their practical work. But he himself often fails to go through those biblical doors to see where the light is leading him. The questions he raises, for instance about the place of responsibility and forgiveness in counselling or the relationship of counselling and preaching, are very important. Anyone concerned to work out a pastoral ministry that is truly biblical must ask the same questions. It is the way Adams answers those questions which is so often disturbing. His claims to a thorough-going biblical position must be regarded as suspect.

Even more importantly, our examination of Adams' position makes us ask a more fundamental question: What does it mean to be 'biblical'? What is a 'biblical pastor'? What is 'biblical counselling'? If Adams leaves us feeling unsatisfied, other writers may help us to find more satisfactory answers to that question.

Notes

1. Adams, Jay, *More than Redemption*, Phillipsburg NJ, Presbyterian & Reformed, 1979
2. Crabb, Lawrence, *Understanding People*, Basingstoke, Marshall Pickering, 1987
3. Hurding, Roger, *Roots and Shoots*, London, Hodder & Stoughton 1986
4. Tidball, Derek, *Skilful Shepherds*, Leicester, IVP, 1986
5. The origins of Nouthetic Counselling are described in the preface to Adams' *Competent to Counsel*, Nutley NJ, Presbyterian & Reformed, 1973

6. *More than Redemption*, p. ix
7. ibid., p. xiii
8. 'Nouthetic Counselling' in Collins, G. R. (Ed.), *Helping People Grow*, Santa Ana, Vision House, 1980, p.155
9. *More than Redemption*, p. 177
10. ibid. pp. 158f
11. cf. Isbister, N. J., 'Are the mind-benders straight?', in *Third Way*, Vol.1, No., 18, pp. 3–6
12. *More than Redemption*, pp. 50f
13. cf. Jones E., *The Life and Work of Sigmund Freud*, Harmondsworth, Penguin, 1964, pp. 89–107
14. *Helping People Grow*, p. 160
15. ibid., p. 163, n13
16. *Basic types of Pastoral Care and Counselling*, London, SCM., 2nd ed. 1984, p. 127
17. *More than Redemption*, p. 234
18. ibid., p. 245
19. Pattison S., A Critique of Pastoral Care, London, SCM., 1988, chapter 6
20. *More than Redemption*, chapter 8
21. ibid., p. 121
22. Calvin, John, *Institutes,* Book 1, xviii, 1
23. *Helping People Grow*, p. 158
24. *More than Redemption*, p. 4
25. ibid, chapter 8
26. Barker M., 'Models of Pastoral Care: Medical, Psychological and Biblical' in Jeeves M.A. (Ed.), *Behavioural Sciences: A Christian Perspective*, Leicester, IVP, 1984, p. 242
27. *More than Redemption*, p. 285
28. ibid., p. 294
29. ibid., chapter 18
30. ibid., p. 272
31. ibid., p. 146
32. ibid., p. 98
33. ibid., p. 151
34. ibid. chapter 18

35. McGrath, A. E., *The Enigma of the Cross*, London, Hodder & Stoughton, 1987, p. 31

36. *More than Redemption*, p. 306

37. ibid., chapter 19

38. ibid., p. 279

39. ibid., appendix

40. For example by Winter R., 'Jay Adams – is he really biblical enough?' in *Third Way*, Vol. 5, No. 4. pp. 9–12

41. *More than Redemption*, p. 284n

42. Barr, J., *The Semantics of Biblical Language*, Oxford, OUP, 1961, p. 159

43. *More than Redemption*, p. 198

2

LAWRENCE CRABB'S
UNDERSTANDING PEOPLE

The Bible as Framework

Lawrence Crabb, like Adams, has pursued a career in theological training in the USA. He is Director of the Institute in Biblical Counselling at Grace Seminary, Ashland, which is also in the Reformed tradition, and has published many books on counselling. If Crabb lacks the clarity and directness of Adams in his writing, he has an ability to explore as well as to engage deeper emotions in the reader. At times this is a very moving book; it would be difficult to describe Adams' *More than Redemption* as moving. A work on pastoral care that fails to engage our emotions may well be considered inadequate, if a Christian understanding of people as wholes is correct. We are not just bodies, still less simply souls. Human beings are a unity of the physical, spiritual and emotional. Much of pastoral care is concerned with the emotional.

There is also a real sense of struggle in Crabb's work. Understanding people is complex, because people are complex, and therefore their problems are complex. 'The temptation to rush quickly to the end of the mystery novel must be resisted.'[1] The Christian life is not straightforward and easy to explain; we experience only a 'marred joy' in this life.[2] And the Christian counsellor may not find the Bible a straightforward book to work with; it does not offer us a 'psychological road map'.[3] This lack of clarity is frustrating, but it is also essentially Christian:

A wise person chooses to walk according to God's revealed plan – 'trust and obey' – but it is soon discovered that living in this world even with the lamp of Scripture can be terribly confusing. God has not made clear how everything works and what is best to do in every situation. When we admit the confusion and *actively enter into it* rather than running from it with pat answers, we are sometimes immobilized by indecision. We just don't know what to do. Strong leaders with definitive answers attract scores of followers who fail to recognize that the confusion they feel is necessary and good: necessary because God has not chosen to answer every question we ask, and good because confusion about what to do and how things make sense presents us with an opportunity to draw deeply from our distinctly human capacity to choose.[4]

This sense of struggle, of readiness to grasp uncertainty, is welcome and refreshing after the somewhat harsh certainties of Adams. It should not be taken as any sign of Crabb's lack of commitment to a thoroughly evangelical doctrine of Scripture. He accepts the authority of the Bible as firmly as Adams; every page of this book assures the reader of his concern to be thoroughly biblical. His *use* of the Bible differs, however, from that of Adams in many ways.

The Bible as a Framework

Crabb rejects two positions taken by Christian counsellors on the use of the Bible. He characterizes these counsellors as 'Stiff exegetes' and 'Self-lovers'.[5] 'Stiff exegetes' must always start with a biblical passage, and keep a distance between Scripture and individual. Scripture always stands over the individual in this stiff exegesis, always there to challenge, rebuke and convict. This ensures the supremacy of the Word of God. But, says Crabb, '[Stiff exegetes] in order to maintain a nonrelational, impersonal understanding of the Bible ... must neglect many passages that underline the importance of community and intimacy.'[6] Although the stiff exegetes' position is very close to being right, in the end it does violence to Scripture and to people. It damages biblical understanding because 'it is possible to give to the literal meaning of the text a comprehensive relevance that it simply does not have'.[7] One might quote as an example of this damage to the biblical revelation Adams' use, mentioned above, of Romans 14:23b as a universal principle that can be applied generally in counselling. It damages people because it is simplistic by narrowing the range of permissible questions to those directly raised in the biblical text; what does that text have to say directly to someone suffering from anorexia, for example? Can one only 'biblically' counsel such a person if one can find a text directly relating to his problem?[8]

'Self-lovers', by contrast, tend to treat modern psychological theory as having the same authority as Scripture. They talk of 'two books', the human sciences and the Bible, and keep the two separate, rather than allowing each to listen to and take account of the other. Both are sources of revelation from God, but the two are synthesized only at the end of a process of expounding each.[9] Crabb objects that this is dangerous to biblical authority. Firstly, this approach retreats from revelation to rationalism, because any conflicts between the two 'books' tend to be resolved by personal judgement. Secondly, it tends to be over-sceptical in practice about the possibility of any objective truth, and therefore leads to empiricism and rationalism.[10]

Crabb offers a third approach to the right use of the Bible in counselling. We must neither regard the Bible as offering detailed prescriptions for counselling, nor regard it as no more than a source of information that is parallel to the insights of human sciences. What Scripture offers counsellors is a *framework* for thinking.[11] It is not in individual texts that the Christian counsellor will find the right way forward, but in the overall doctrinal framework that the Bible provides. 'Biblical data support doctrinal categories which have implications that comprehensively deal with every relational issue of life.'[12] A truly Christian approach to counselling can be derived from the Bible – indeed, it must be if it is to be truly Christian – but it is derived indirectly, by meditating on biblical doctrine, rather than by

using individual passages or books as rules for the conduct of counselling. Creating such a Christian approach will involve a struggle
with the Bible; an easy reading of principles off the page will not be
possible.

This approach of Crabb looks promising, but at times he seems to
undermine his own position by his lack of clarity. Having apparently
rejected the idea of a Christian counselling emerging directly from
the Bible, he still states that 'counselling models must demonstrate
more than mere consistency with Scripture; they must in fact
emerge from it'.[13] Here he seems unaware of the fact that 'counselling models' cannot, by definition, emerge from the Bible,
because 'counselling' is a modern concept, and not a biblical one.
Guidelines for our counselling may emerge from the Bible, but
specific 'counselling models' never will, because there is no 'counselling' in the Bible.

He also appears to want to hold on to the idea of the Bible as a
'textbook' for Christian counselling. The Bible is sufficient because
'it is a textbook for relational living',[14] and all human problems stem
ultimately from relationships, supremely from our broken relationship with God. Crabb does recognize a problem here: 'Is the Bible a
counselling textbook? The answer we give will depend on how we
define counselling.'[15] This really does seem confused. Presumably he
is saying that the Bible itself would not equate counselling with
psychotherapy as understood in the twentieth century; but that is to
assume a 'biblical' definition of counselling before going to the Bible.
Of course the Bible does not equate counselling and psychotherapy,
because it knows nothing of either – both are modern ideas. Crabb
also seems to be confused about the nature of a textbook. The Bible
is only a counselling textbook if we also redefine what we mean by
'textbook'. A cursory glance at Scripture will tell even the inexperi-
enced reader that it bears no relation to any textbook she may have
on her bookshelves. The minimum of involvement with biblical
scholarship will assure us, and Crabb, that 'textbook' is not one of
the literary categories found in the Bible. Even when it looks as if it
might be a textbook, in the books of Kings, the author specifically
reminds us it is not. He deliberately refers us to other works for a

full chronicle of the history whose *theological* importance he is concerned to elucidate (e.g. 1 Kings 16:5, 14, 20, 27).

Crabb's endorsement of the idea of the Bible as providing the counsellor with an authoritative framework within which to develop a truly Christian approach to counselling is helpful. It does indeed avoid extremes of biblicism and rationalism. But we need to do more work on how to move from framework to system.

The Bible and Human Sciences

Crabb's understanding of the Bible as a framework, and not a simple prescription for the Christian counsellor, leaves him room to take a moderately positive approach to the human sciences. It is simply not Christian to shut the door to other points of view, because we believe in the Creator God, who sustains the universe and is at work in all of it, continuing his creating work even in and through those who do not acknowledge him as the Lord of the universe. We need to articulate our own position clearly, but also 'maintain a willing openness to changing positions ... self-consciously labour to walk the tightrope of open conviction.'[16] It is positively damaging to ignore the questions put to us by the researches of human scientists: 'A biblical model for explaining human behaviour will never be embarrassed by the data of human behaviour; we should therefore bring to the model honest questions that we are forced to ask as we work with people. Every genuine enquiry should stimulate hard thinking which will expand, refine, or contradict the model, but which always reflects a prior commitment to biblical authority.'[17] One of Crabb's closing reflections in the book is that some secular therapy may be less harmful than some so-called 'biblical counselling', because it does attempt to plumb the depths of the human character and condition. 'Biblical counselling', by contrast, may damage people by trying to force their situation and problems into an artificial framework, which denies the whole reality of what they are facing.

The theological basis for this position is that God does reveal himself in Creation, although the purpose of his revelation in

Creation is, says Crabb, limited. The Creation teaches us that we must reckon with a Creator, but the Bible 'tells us how to find life,'[18] and the concern of counselling is with this life. The Bible is plain, because it is propositional in a way that nature is not, and the Bible is unaffected by the sin which has cursed nature.[19]

Crabb explains how this works in practice:

Studying the thinking of other people, whether Christian or not, can be legitimately provocative. The data and theories of psychology can serve as catalysts, stimulating us to consider new directions in our thinking. Both our power of reasoning and our intuition must be permitted a role in our efforts to build a counselling model. But in all that we do, the Bible must provide the *framework* within which we work, and the *premises* from which we draw our conclusions.[20]

Once again I find Crabb helpful on this point, but his position is spoilt by his lack of clarity. What he seems to be saying is that the superiority of the Bible's revelation to the revelation in Creation is assured because we have been promised the Holy Spirit's help in understanding Scripture, but this help is not given to the scientist.[21] What does Crabb mean here? Does he mean that the Christian working in any field of science is not indwelt by the Holy Spirit, or somehow has less of the Holy Spirit than the pastor poring over a biblical passage as he sits at his desk preparing his sermon for Sunday? We need to hear more from Crabb, I think, on the limits of scientific endeavour, and, more importantly, on the work of the Holy Spirit. How does he work to keep God's people in the truth? He is surely at work in the world and the Church, and not just in the individual Christian before his Bible.

In the same section of his book, Crabb also seems rather confused about the nature of authority: 'Although we may regard the ideas of psychology as stimulating and catalytic, we may never regard them as authoritative.'[22] But what does 'authoritative' mean here? Crabb does not seem to be aware of a problem in his use of the word. Is 'theology' more authoritative than 'science'? Are the biochemistry and dietetics books on my wife's bookshelves less authoritative than the theology books on mine? Because most of my books have a strong element of speculation and interpretation in them, they may well be more provisional in their conclusions, they may well be less authoritative in some senses than my wife's books. Her books contain an element of speculation and interpretation, but in the main deal with straightforward description. And they certainly do not attempt to explain the nature of God or human destiny, matters on which any human opinion must always be provisional, because the truth will only finally be known when we stand in the presence of God himself. The Bible does indeed explain the nature of God and human destiny, but it does not explain everything about them. There are still mysteries that will be unfolded to human minds only on the last day. What has been unfolded to us in the Scriptures is enough for us to respond truly to God in this life; even that will always be read through my own sinful understanding.

We need to remember, then, that the Bible has an appropriate authority, although we shall always remain humble about the extent to which we have grasped its authoritative teaching, and also that scientific statements have their own authority; we have to acknowledge their appropriate authority as well. The human sciences may include a greater element of subjective speculation and interpretation than, say, biochemistry, but the conclusions of human scientists still have an appropriate authority. As Christians who believe in a God who has created human beings and sustains their life by his power, we cannot ignore the authoritative statements of those who research into human nature and experience, or undermine their authority by reducing it to a 'provocative' role.

A Biblical Anthropology

If understanding the Bible involves a struggle, Crabb also assures us that it will not be easy to arrive at a biblical understanding of human nature. He rejects overly simplistic models of personhood, and seeks to hold together diverse elements in biblical teaching. He sees the balance as holding together three elements:

- First of all, Christian counsellors need to remember that every human being bears the image of God: 'Counsellors must recognize that the clients they are trying to help bear the image of God. No other fact is more significant and necessary to a proper under-standing of people.'[23]

- But Crabb does not have an idealistic understanding of human nature. Human beings are infected by sin, which touches not just the surface of human beings, but is deep-seated.[24]

- However, this sin does not erase the image of God in people, it only mars it.

It is essential that this balance be held in our understanding of people. Crabb sums it up by describing even the best of human experiences as offering only a 'marred joy'.[25] It is vital that we recognize the depths of human nature; too much Christian counselling concentrates on behaviour, and ignores the innermost being and the thirsty soul of which the Bible so often speaks. In this respect Freud is near to the truth than some Christian writers.[26] People are not just dynamic, controlled by their past experiences, nor simply moral, to be judged by their own behaviour. They are personal, rational, voli-tional, emotional, relational. All these elements must be taken into account by the Christian counsellor. The second half of the book is concerned with Crabb's exposition of these aspects of human personality.

Crabb offers us a realistic and helpful understanding of person-hood. If there is a flaw in his exposition it is that he tends to see people in a very individualistic fashion. Crabb sees the aim of coun-selling as repentance and obedience, not on the surface, but after deep layers of wrong choices have been exposed.[27] He acknowledges that people may well have been damaged by past experiences, espe-cially at the hands of their parents. The student who comes to talk about his problems in facing up to his girlfriend's expectation of a relationship leading to a real commitment may not have problems with his girlfriend. The astute pastor will want to dig deeper to discover what image of commitment and relationship has been left buried in the deep places of his personality by his experience of family life. Here Crabb has much to teach us, but he nowhere acknowledges that an individual may have problems because of the failure of the social structure in which that person is set. The perceptive pastor spending time with a young mother who feels depressed, will be very aware that her accommodation, in a flat on the sixteenth floor of a tower block where the lift is frequently out of order, plays a major part in her problem. The pastoral task for this pastor is not only to offer support to the individual but to attempt to challenge the sinful structures which have left her isolated.

Crabb emphasizes the importance of the relational aspect of human personhood, but fails to go on to explore how this has been damaged by sin in the widest sense. He regularly emphasizes the importance of healthy church life, but seems to forget about that when he starts talking about counselling again. He makes the mistake that appears too common in works on counselling, of equating the pastoral task with ministry to the individual. Although there are great differences between Crabb and Adams, we are in this book once again faced with pastoral work as consisting, in essence, of dealing with the problems of particular people. The Bible sees people in much less strongly individualistic terms; a truly biblical pastoral theology will also do so.

Notes

1. *Understanding People*, p. 78
2. ibid., p. 125
3. ibid., p. 134
4. ibid., p. 169
5. ibid., p. 9
6. ibid., p. 10
7. ibid., p. 55
8. ibid., p. 57
9. cf. Crabb's diagram on p.38
10. ibid., p. 37–42
11. ibid., p. 29

12. ibid., p. 63
13. ibid., p. 29
14. ibid., p. 62
15. ibid., p. 59
16. ibid., p. 15
17. ibid., p. 193
18. ibid., p. 42
19. ibid., p. 43
20. ibid., p. 44
21. ibid.
22. ibid.
23. ibid., p. 122
24. ibid., p. 124
25. ibid., p. 125
26. ibid., p. 61
27. ibid., p. 124

3

ROGER HURDING'S
ROOTS AND SHOOTS

The Bible as Touchstone

Roger Hurding is an English doctor, who had to leave general practice as a result of the limitations caused by diabetes. Moving into
student health work, he began to develop an interest in counselling,
which he has practised in recent years in close connection with
Christ Church, Clifton, a very large Anglican congregation in
Bristol. Hurding has told his life story in *As Trees Walking*.[1] and his
aims as a Christian counsellor have been set out in *Restoring the
Image*,[2] and also some more popular works. (These include a valuable
contribution to the subject of this book in *The Bible and Counselling*,[3]
but I have deliberately ignored that book in what follows, since I
want to try to understand *Roots and Shoots* on its own terms.)

In considering *Roots and Shoots* it needs to be said that the aim of
the book in itself demands a different response from that offered to
Adams and Crabb. Hurding is not attempting to justify one particular approach to counselling as 'biblical' as compared with other
systems. He wants rather to survey the whole world of psychology
and psychotherapy since Freud, and to offer an assessment of that
world through Christian, biblical eyes. The style of the book also
provokes a different response; Hurding is sympathetic rather than
polemical. The whole book breathes a spirit which could be
described as 'pastoral'. The most obvious epithet for Adams' work
is, perhaps, 'confrontational', and for Crabb's 'emotional'.

Hurding also displays a quite remarkable breadth of reading – this
really is something of a Cook's Tour of counselling. It is remarkable

especially as Hurding has had several problems with his eyesight, including two periods of blindness, resulting from his diabetes. The work is meticulously referenced – that, in itself, is an object lesson to Adams – and so presents a useful introduction to the subject for anyone coming to it for the first time. Hurding shows less evidence of wide reading in the field of biblical theology, but he is no mean theologian. He has obviously reaped the benefit of working within a church with a very competent teaching ministry. I am not in a position to offer a critique of the strictly psychological elements in Hurding's work, but several aspects of his use of the Bible should be noted.

Hermeneutical Sagacity

This, says Hurding, is what Christians who enter the world of counselling need. They must avoid a knee-jerk text quotation when faced with some system or statement which, at first sight, appears to conflict with the biblical picture. They must be prepared to go deeper. Evangelicals too easily react against statements by quoting biblical texts. A particular counselling system is based around the idea of careful listening to the person who comes seeking help. Christians can too easily reject such a form of counselling by quoting 'Proclaim the message; be persistent whether the time is favourable or unfavourable; convince, rebuke and encourage' (2 Timothy 4:2a). People who come for help need to hear God's Word proclaimed to them; simply to listen to them is clearly inadequate. But is that all that the Bible has to say? The last few words of 2 Timothy 4:2 immediately shed a slightly different light on the question – '... with the utmost patience in teaching.' Jesus' own style – teaching the small group of apostles very thoroughly over a long period whilst spending time with them, responding to their questions, proclaiming the Kingdom to the crowds whilst also being aware of the individual in need at their heart – reflects this balance perfectly. A careful consideration of the whole of the Scriptures, and of the aims of the counselling system concerned, may well produce a very different response.

Hurding rejects the idea of the Bible as a textbook. It is not, he says, quoting Richard Lovelace, 'a compendium of all necessary knowledge',[4] but rather 'a touchstone for testing and verifying other kinds of truth and a structure for integrating them.' We cannot simply turn up the answer to every problem in the pages of Scripture. But the Bible does reveal God's ways to us. It helps us to understand and evaluate the many different ideas and theories presented to us as human knowledge expands, but it does not tell us everything we need to know about every aspect of life. Hurding clearly has a very high view of the authority and inspiration of Scripture, but this does not lead him into a simplistic use of biblical verses.

Special and General Revelation

Hurding is concerned that, in any evaluation of a counselling methodology, due weight should be given to both special revelation and general revelation. Special revelation is the Word of God as revealed in the Scriptures. General revelation is the truth discovered through observation of the world and in the process of history. There must be a balance between the two, each in its proper place. Therefore, when considering questions of psychology, there is a place for both deductive reasoning – arguing 'from the top down' – and inductive reasoning – arguing 'from the bottom up'. Is Hurding here simply replicating what Crabb calls a 'two books' theory of revelation? I think not, because Hurding carefully underlines that special revelation is *special*; it speaks of God with a clarity which general revelation cannot, and it speaks of God's 'remedial' work in Christ, which general revelation does not.[5]

Hurding does not attempt to develop this pattern at any great length, but the whole book is based on a balanced approach to revelation. This seems to do justice to the Bible's picture of God, who has both created the world and has spoken to the world in the pages of Scripture. God has not abandoned the world which he created; he continues to sustain it, and to do his creative and recreative work in it. And he has not stopped speaking to his world; he still enables men and women to understand his will by giving his Holy Spirit to help them interpret the Bible correctly.

Biblical Anthropology

Hurding suggests an outline of a biblical anthropology as part of the framework necessary for a genuinely Christian assessment of psychological theories.[6] There are five elements to this framework:

- As human beings we have supreme value.
- We have this value because we have been created in the image of God.
- Because we are in God's image, we are living unities, whole personalities.
- We also have broken relationships with God, with the created order, and with others.
- However, we are restorable to Christ.

This seems to be a framework which is in accord both with the picture of the whole of Scripture, and with many of the insights gained in modern psychology. At the same time it profoundly challenges many other aspects of psychological systems. It is balanced and biblical.

As Hurding also points out, a biblical anthropology is not just theory, it is fleshed out in the Incarnation. As Christians we have not only a theory of human nature, but also a model of human nature, Jesus Christ himself. There is a christological centre to both general and special revelation. This must be the Christian understanding, although many evangelical Christians give the impression that the key to understanding revelation is some concept derived from the Pauline writings, rather than Jesus Christ himself. How often do Christian counsellors, pastors and theologians work with such a balanced, Christ-centred picture of human beings?

Eclecticism

One of the most marked features of Hurding's work is his refusal to ally himself to any one system of psychotherapeutic or counselling theory as *the* 'Christian' system. He will neither set himself up wholly against or wholly for any system. Hurding is, in this area, a risk-taker. He refuses to seek security in one particular methodology. He is unhappy both with Christian attempts to assimilate humanistic psychology, and with those who react totally against such systems. His concern is for a continued dialogue between the two. This dialogue must be genuinely two-way, with theology willing to speak out, and not just be swamped by or ignore secular systems.[7]

In his own practice Hurding clearly favours an eclectic approach. He attempts to draw out what is best in different methodologies, and to use the appropriate technique for each client.[8] The student with a clear academic understanding cannot be approached in the same way as the elderly person, with a much richer experience of life, but less formal education. The teenage girl who appears to be sleeping around and even getting pregnant as an attention-seeking device, because no one has ever truly cared for her, demands a different technique in counselling from the sixth-former who has over-indulged at a party and ended up in bed with someone else's boyfriend. He himself has experience of training in a number of different techniques.

This discerning eclecticism shows itself in other areas as well. Although Hurding is quite clearly an evangelical, he shows an openness to insights in Catholic spirituality. As he points out, Christ cannot be narrowed down – he is prophet, pastor, priest and paraclete – and his salvation cannot be narrowed down either – it is an experience of repentance, restoration, reconciliation, redemption and regeneration.[9] The richness of Christ's work demands a richness in our response to him, and in all our work for him. In the light of Christ and the breadth of his work we could therefore be foolish, and less than Christian, to attempt to narrow down what is offered in counselling to a single system. 'God's revelation, in both Word and created order, with respect to caring for one another, is somehow wider than the constraints of one particular methodology of counselling'.[10] Those seem to me to be words of some wisdom. Indeed, Hurding's whole approach, careful but not afraid to challenge, seems to inject into the world of counselling, and particularly Christian counselling, a wisdom which is often, sadly, absent.

Notes

1. Hurding, Roger, *As Trees Walking*, Exeter, Paternoster, 1982
2. Exeter, Paternoster, 1980
3. London, Hodder & Stoughton, 1992
4. *Roots and Shoots*, p. 306
5. ibid., p. 258–61
6. ibid., chapter 11
7. ibid., chapter 10
8. ibid., chapter 11
9. ibid., chapter 16
10. ibid., p. 290

DEREK TIDBALL'S
SKILFUL SHEPHERDS

The Bible as Foundation

Derek Tidball is a Baptist minister who has taught at the London Bible College and pastored a large church in Plymouth. More recently he has held a major executive position with the English Baptist Union, before his latest appointment in which he returns to the London Bible College as Principal. He has also written *An Introduction to the Sociology of the New Testament.*[1] He is essentially a theologian with a concern for pastoral practice and the human sciences, and so the direction of his book is the opposite to Hurding's; it is essentially deductive − from theology 'down' to pastoral practice − rather than inductive. We should also note that *Skilful Shepherds* is not just a book about counselling. Christian pastoral work is not just about individuals with problems, it is a far broader task, touching on the whole life and witness of the local church. Simply by making that point Tidball sends a vitally important message to Christian counsellors.

Part One of *Skilful Shepherds* looks at the biblical foundations for pastoral theology, with a very wide-ranging study of biblical material. Part Two is a historical survey of pastoral thinking in Christian history, with, in Part Three, a consideration of certain key themes for contemporary pastoral care. The major weakness of the book is probably in Part Two, where there are certain large omissions. There is nothing, for instance, about post-Tridentine Catholic pastoral thinking; one would expect at least a passing reference to the Curé d'Ars in such an historical survey, although one is grateful for Tidball's introduction to so many key characters in the history of pastoral theology. A further weakness is that this section is not really integrated into Parts One and Three. It is, however, an important section, because it shows that Tidball is aware of being within a great historical tradition of pastoral theology. It also shows the weakness of modern evangelical pastoral theology, which is almost nonexistent except in the area of counselling. What, then, are the marks of Tidball's work?

The Pre-eminence of Scripture

Tidball's theology is thoroughly evangelical in asserting the pre-eminence of Scripture, and pointing out the dangers of allowing that pre-eminence to be abandoned. The pastoral situation must be clearly grasped, but it must be seen in the light of Scripture. As he says in commenting on Hiltner's work: 'The shepherding perspective may well inform and question the theology but more fundamentally the theology will inform and question the work of the shepherd and that relationship must not be reversed.'[2]

If we assert the pre-eminence of Scripture, then our pastoral theology will be genuinely Christian, because it will be pointed by Scripture to its true centre in Christ, and it will always be marked by the pre-eminence of the Gospel. As Tidball points out, the greatest danger to evangelicalism is always its tendency to slip into pharisaism, slipping away from the Gospel and into law.[3] We can only avoid that by holding on to the *whole* message of the Scriptures, not allowing ourselves to concentrate simply on those parts of it which we happen to know or which appeal directly to our own personalities. Asserting the pre-eminence of Scripture demands a commitment to the Bible as a whole, and not just to one part of it. That was the mistake of the Pharisees, with their close attention to the laws of the Old Testament, and their failure to pay equally close attention to the message of the prophets and the liberating words of Jesus himself. Too many Christians make the same mistake today.

Careful Biblical Exegesis

Tidball is prepared to engage in the hard work which produces successful biblical exegesis. In the first part of his book he shows how the biblical record has much to say about contemporary pastoral situations. In Part Three he works back from contemporary themes to see how whole books of the Bible deal with parallel themes in their own situation. In all this he refuses to deal with the Bible at the level of single verses or a few key passages, but rather looks at whole books, or at least lengthy sections of books, to see the Scriptures in their own context and to apply them carefully to our contemporary context. Few evangelical pastoral writers demonstrate such care in their handling of the Bible; it is to be hoped that the revival of evangelical biblical scholarship over the last twenty years will bear fruit in the area of pastoral theology as well. Much evangelical exegesis of Scripture is poor because evangelicals have been poorly taught in this area until comparatively recently. Tidball sets an example of creative dialogue between pastoral theology and biblical scholarship, which needs to be imitated widely.

Refusal to Systematize

As Tidball constantly points out, the Bible does not offer us a simple pastoral structure or programme. Pastoral leadership in Israel is neither static nor monolithic, and the New Testament picture is even more fluid. There are clear principles underlying the Bible's vision of the pastoral task, but these do not harden into a system. That same refusal to systematize should mark our pastoral theology as well, or we are in danger of failing to take real pastoral situations seriously. Because such situations concern real people in all their complexity, they cannot be fitted into a neat framework. Pastoral Theology is not an enemy of Systematic Theology, but it does want to challenge it by forcing it to face up to the contradictions of real human experience. 'It is doubtful if a systematic method, in the modern academic sense, is appropriate to a theology which is pastoral.'[4]

A Broad Task

As we have already noted, the breadth of Tidball's biblical under-standing prevents him from narrowing down the pastoral task. The Bible will not allow us to think that pastoring involves simply coun-selling and dealing with problems. Tidball gives much space to 'problem areas', as is natural, but his concern to retain the biblical breadth of pastoral concern keeps breaking through. There is space in his work for such issues as liberation theology, the nurture of the healthy and the priestly role of the minister, not matters always dealt with by evangelical pastoral writers – or, for that matter, by those of other traditions. His vision challenges much modern thinking and practice, not least amongst his fellow evangelicals.

English and American Attitudes

It is interesting to see how Tidball and Hurding, writing at almost the same time and within the same English evangelical scene, although from within different denominations, both demonstrate a broad sympathy in their understanding of the pastoral task, even though their particular fields are different. It may be that their English context influences the way in which they approach their subject, just as Adams' and Crabb's American context affected their writing. Both Adams and, to a lesser extent, Crabb appear to be writing for American evangelicals who have been influenced by a fundamentalism which is strongly suspicious of science. Science teaches evolution, which is at odds with Genesis 1; science teaches geology, which is at odds with the Genesis account of a universal flood. Science attacks the biblical account of human origins and, by implication, a Christian understanding of human nature. As a result science is seen as one of the great enemies of the true, biblical Christian faith. And, if physical sciences are dangerous, human sciences are even more dangerous, and must be resisted all the more strongly. In Britain there has never been such a division between Christianity and science, if only because so many scientists have been evangelical Christians. As a result there has not been such a distrust of science in the evangelical community, and writers such as Hurding and Tidball can approach the human sciences more openly.

It also appears that Adams and Crabb both need to present us with a 'system' of counselling. Unless we are offered such a system, we are not in a position to say that what we are doing is 'biblical'. This again may be a reflection of the American scene against which they teach and write, a scene which has tended to define orthodoxy as a commitment to a system. It will be obvious to the reader by now that I do not consider that it is possible to extract a system for pastoral care from the Bible. The Bible itself, as we have seen, is not systematic. Many years ago, when I was an undergraduate, the distinguished New Testament scholar George Caird taught us that biblical theology must be understood as a 'conference'. The different authors of Scripture sit round one table and, from their different viewpoints, contribute their understanding of God and his work in history. There is a unity here, because they do indeed sit round one table, and talk of the same God, the same Christ, the same Holy Spirit. Thus there is one Bible. But that Bible contains a great diversity of methods by which, and viewpoints from which, the story is told. The Bible itself, therefore, is not systematic, and neither can pastoral situations be systematized. Pastoral situations deal with the responses, emotions and behaviour of people, as individuals and as groups. Such behaviour always has an element of unpredictability about it, simply because it is the behaviour of people and not of machines. Whilst we can get help in understanding those responses from those who have studied human behaviour and undertaken the pastoral task before us, each situation must be carefully listened to and understood for itself, if we are to take it seriously.

Hurding and Tidball, therefore, offer a more promising approach to the pastoral task by their refusal to systematize. When the Bible is used as a touchstone by which to assess pastoral methods offered to us, and as a foundation undergirding all that we do, then we are able to put the right questions to pastoral situations and respond to them in a way that is not contrary to Scripture. We do not have to work our way through the situation according to one particular route map in order to be biblical, but we do have to keep the range of biblical questions and models constantly in our minds.

It may be that Hurding's and Tidball's more open attitude to both the human sciences and the nature of Scripture offers an opportunity for the revival of something that has been semi-dormant since the days of the Puritans, a genuinely English evangelical pastoral theology.[5]

Notes

1. Tidball, Derek, *An Introduction to the Sociology of the New Testament*, Exeter, Paternoster, 1983
2. *Skilful Shepherds*, p. 24
3. ibid., chapter 14
4. ibid., p. 248
5. I use the word 'English' advisedly. Pastoral theology has flourished in Scotland for centuries.

EPILOGUE

TOWARDS AN EVANGELICAL
PASTORAL THEOLOGY

Throughout the writing of this book, and especially Part Four, I have been aware of some cautionary words of Crabb: 'Christian counsellors devote a good deal of their writing and lecturing to denouncing other Christian counsellors as unbiblical in their views, or at least not as biblical as themselves.'[1] It would be easy to be unfair to others in a desire to promote one's own position, and, as we know, one's own position is always more sensible and more Christian than anyone else's. I hope I have been fair to each of the authors considered, even though I have not examined them all in the same detail.

Crabb's words should not, however, distract us from the work of examining claims to be biblical. The task of using the Bible well is too important for us to allow shoddy work to go unchallenged. Too many people have been damaged by the pastoral misuse of the Bible for any of us in pastoral ministry to be complacent about the way we use it ourselves. The Bible is pastoral and theological. It tells us about God, and it deals with human situations. The Church, which claims to live under the authority of the Bible, must hold these two together. All four of the books which we have considered in this final part show a common concern to do just that, although, as will be clear, I believe Adams does so far less successfully than do the others – the amount of space allotted to each one does not reflect in any way my judgement of their respective importance; it does, to a certain extent, reflect what may be their relative circulation amongst pastors. I suspect Adams' clear certainties are more appealing to evangelical pastors than the more complex picture painted by the others.

Christ's promise to his people is that his truth will set us free, and his truth is indivisible. It is theological and pastoral; he wants his people to be biblically sound and pastorally whole. Such a balance is not always easy to maintain. It needs careful dialogue between biblical theologians and human scientists, it needs pastors who are also theologians, biblical scholars who are also pastors, so that the Church can maintain its biblical balance, pastoral and theological.

Note

1. Crabb, Lawrence, *Understanding People*, p. 7

SUGGESTED FURTHER READING

Parts 1 and 2

Ballard, P., (Ed.), *The Foundations of Pastoral Studies and Practical Theology*, Cardiff, HOLI 4, 1986

Bridger, F., & Atkinson, D., *Counselling in Context*, London, Marshall Pickering, HarperCollins, 1994

Campbell, A. V., *Rediscovering Pastoral Care*, London, DLT, 2nd ed., 1986

Clinebell, H., *Basic Types of Pastoral Care and Counselling*, London SCM, 2nd ed., 1984

Cotterell, P., *Mission and Meaninglessness*, London, SPCK, 1990

Deeks, D., *Pastoral Theology: An Inquiry*, London, Epworth, 1987

Finney, J., *The Well Church Book*, Warwick, CPAS & London, SU, 1991

Green, L., *Power to the Powerless*, Basingstoke, Marshall, Morgan & Scott, 1987

— *Let's do Theology*, London, Mowbray, 1990

Greidanus, S., *The Modern Preacher and the Ancient Text*, Grand Rapids, Eerdmans, & Leicester, IVP, 1988

Jacobs, M., (Ed.), *Faith or Fear?*, London, DLT, 1987

Leonard, G., *God Alive – Priorities in Pastoral Theology*, London, DLT, 1981

Oates, W., (Ed.), *An Introduction to Pastoral Counselling*, Nashville, Broadman, 1959

O'Donovan, O, *Resurrection and Moral Order*, Leicester, IVP, 1986

Oglesby, W., Jr, *Biblical Themes for Pastoral Care*, Nashville, Abingdon, 1980

Pattison, S., *A Critique of Pastoral Care*, London, SCM, 1988

Peterson, E. H., *The Contemplative Pastor*, Grand Rapids, Eerdmans, 1993 (published as *The Gift*, London, Marshall Pickering, 1995)

— *Working the Angles*, Grand Rapids, Eerdmans, 1993

— *Five Smooth Stones for Pastoral Work*, Atlanta, John Knox, 1980

Stott, J. R. W., *I Believe in Preaching*, London, Hodder & Stoughton, 1982

Thiselton, A. C., *The Two Horizons*, Exeter, Paternoster, 1980

Willimon, W. H., *Worship as Pastoral Care*, Nashville, Abingdon, 1979

There are three major dictionaries of pastoral care:

Atkinson, D. J., & Field, D. H., (Eds.), *New Dictionary of Christian Ethics and Pastoral Theology*, Leicester & Downers Grove, IVP, 1995

Campbell, A. V. (Ed.), *A Dictionary of Pastoral Care*, London, SPCK, 1987

Hunter, R. J., (Eds.), *Dictionary of Pastoral Care and Counselling*, Nashville, Abingdon, 1990

Part 3

Commentaries on the Corinthian Epistles

Barrett, C. K., *1 Corinthians*, London, A. & C. Black, 2nd ed., 1971

— *2 Corinthians*, London, A. & C. Black, 1973

Bruce, F. F., *1 & 2 Corinthians*, London, Marshall, Morgan & Scott, 1971

Conzelmann, H., *1 Corinthians*, Philadelphia, Fortress, 1975

Prior, D., *The Message of 1 Corinthians*, Leicester, IVP, 1985

Commentaries on Jeremiah

Harrison, R. K., *Jeremiah and Lamentations*, London, Tyndale, 1973

Holladay, W. L., *Jeremiah*, 2 vols, Philadelphia & Minneapolis, Fortress, 1986, 1989

Kidner, D., *The Message of Jeremiah*, Leicester, IVP, 1987

McConville, J. G., *Judgement and Promise*, Leicester, Apollos, 1993

Thompson, J. A., *The Book of Jeremiah*, Grand Rapids, Eerdmans, 1980

Part 4

Books by Jay Adams

The Christian Counsellor's Manual, Phillipsburg, Presbyterian & Reformed, 1973

Competent to Counsel, Phillipsburg, Presbyterian & Reformed, 1970

Lectures on Counselling, Grand Rapids, Baker, 1978

Matters of Concern to Christian Counsellors, Edinburgh, Christian World, 1977

A Theology of Christian Counselling: More than Redemption, Grand Rapids, Zondervan, 1979

Ready to Restore, Phillipsburg, Presbyterian & Reformed, 1981

Shepherding God's Flock, Phillipsburg, Presbyterian & Reformed, 1975
  vol. 1 – *The Pastoral Life*
  vol. 2 – *Pastoral Counselling*
  vol. 3 – *Pastoral Leadership*

Books by Lawrence Crabb

Basic Principles of Biblical Counselling, Grand Rapids, Zondervan, 1975

Effective Biblical Counselling, Grand Rapids, Zondervan, 1977

Inside Out, Amersham-on-the-Hill, Scripture Press, 1990

Understanding People, Basingstoke, Marshall Pickering, 1988

Men and Women, London, Marshall Pickering, 1995

Be Strong, Be Courageous, London, Marshall Pickering, 1995

Books by Roger Hurding

As Trees Walking, Exeter, Paternoster, 1980

Coping with Illness, London, Hodder & Stoughton, 1988

Restoring the Image, Exeter, Paternoster, 1980

Roots and Shoots, London, Hodder & Stoughton, 1986

The Bible and Counselling, London, Hodder & Stoughton, 1984

Understanding Adolescence, London, Hodder & Stoughton, 1989

Books by Derek Tidball

Introduction to the Sociology of the New Testament, Exeter, Paternoster, 1983

Skilful Shepherds, Leicester, IVP, 1986

INDEX OF SCRIPTURE REFERENCES

Old Testament

REFERENCE	PAGE	REFERENCE	PAGE
Genesis 1	133	**Proverbs** 8:30–31	68
1–3	141		
4	133	**Isaiah** 2:2–4	109
		6:1–10	96
Deuteronomy		13–23	118
12:5–7, 14,21	109	14:32	109
14:23	109	17:12–14	109
16:16	109	28:14–19a	109
32:6	89	29:5–8	109
		32:5f.	90
1 Samuel 3	96	40:21–26	68
3:13	140	40:29	44
		45	131
2 Samuel 12:5–7, 13	62	53	90
1 Kings 16:5, 14, 20, 27	150	**Jeremiah** 1:1–19	96–99
		2:30a	104
2 Kings 21	109	3:11–12	111
		3:14	117
Psalms 119:11	72	3:16	104, 110
		4:4	110

REFERENCE	PAGE	REFERENCE	PAGE
Jeremiah 4:10	104	19:5–6	109
5:1–9	110	20:1ff	102
5:30–31	111	20:7–18	98
6:10	103, 110	21:12	110
6:13–15	111	22:1ff.	110
6:20	110	22:15–16	110
7:1–29	110	23:3	117
7:1ff.	104	23:9–40	111
7:3–11	110	23:10–14	110
7:30–34	109	23:23–4	118
8:18–22	105	24:1–10	112
8:19a	104	25:15–38	118
9:2	103	26	102
9:25–26	104, 110	26:1–15	110
10:11–13	118	26:16–24	95
10:17–22	111	27:1–11	118
11:1–14	110	27:12–22	112
11:11–12	111	28	104
11:15	110	28:1–17	111
11:18–23	98	29:1–32	120, 131
11:20	107	29:1–23	112
12:1–4	98	29:7	104, 120
12:5–13	98	31:1–3	112, 116
14:11–12	110	31:7	117
14:13–15	111	31:10	116
14:19–22	105	31:23–24	116
15:15–19	98f.	31:27–34	115
16:1–4	98	31:31–34	112, 116
17:1–13a	117	31:33–34	110
17:14–18	98, 103	32:1–15	98
17:16	95	32:34–35	109
17:19ff.	110	33:14–26	116
18:5–10	118	34:8–22	115
18:18	98	36:1–3	111
18:19–23	98, 103	36:23–24	102

REFERENCE	PAGE	REFERENCE	PAGE
Jeremiah 37:2	102	**Ezekiel** 1–3	96
38	102	18:1–32	115
38:1–6	98	25–32	118
38:7–28	98	33:1–20	115
40:1–6	103	34	95
40:2–3a	106		
46–51	118	**Amos** 1:2–2:16	118
46:10	119	7:14–15	96
46:26	119		
46:27–28	119	**Jonah**	133
47:6	119		
48:11–17	119		
48:13	111		
48:29	119		
48:47	119		
49:6	119		
49:11	119		
49:39	119		
50	112		
50:3–4	119		
50:14	119		
50:16	119		
50:38	119		
51	112		
51:11	119		
52	112		

New Testament

REFERENCE	PAGE	REFERENCE	PAGE
Matthew 5:45	131	3:1–2	89
		3:5–6	86, 87
Mark 10:45	86	3:11	10
		3:11–15	86
Luke 23:32–43	48–50	3:16	30
		4:4–5	86
John 1–14	65	4:8	82
3:16	68	4:10–13	82, 83
4:24	36	4:14–15	86, 88
5:17	68	4:16	83
14:6	65	4:17	82, 89
18:38	65	5:1–5	84
		5:9–10	89
Acts 20:31	140	6:12	84
		6:15	81
Romans 1:18–32	135	7:1	84
7	72	7:10	85
8:18–23	134	7:12	85
8:31–39	46–48	7:14	132
12:2	72	7:25	84, 85
14:23, 31	135, 148	8:1	84, 85, 89
		9:16	86
1 Corinthians 1:3	82	9:22	85
1:4–9	84	10:23–24	89
1:9	82	11:2–16	84
1:11	81	11:22	87
1:23	82	11:26	85
1:24	82, 86	12	87
1:26	86	12:4–6	82
1:26–29	87	12:7	87
2:10	82	12:14–25	87
3	89	12:28	59

REFERENCE	PAGE	REFERENCE	PAGE
1 Corinthians 12:31	85	12:14	86, 88
13	89	12:18	81
14	89	12:19	89
14:18	85	13:1	81
14:23–25	89	13:10	89
15	45f., 82	13:14	82
15:10	86		
16:5–11,17	81,87	Galatians 5:25	24
16:15–18	87		
		Ephesians 4:11	58, 80
2 Corinthians 1:2f.	82		
1:7	84	Colossians 1:28	7, 63
1:13–24	85	3	132
1:19	82		
3:2–3	84	1 Thessalonians 2:7	89
3:6	86	2:13	30
3:17	82		
4:5	82, 84, 86	2 Thessalonians 2:6	132
4:8–10	83		
5:1	89	1 Timothy	59
5:9–10	86	4:3–5	133
5:10–11	86		
5:14	86	2 Timothy 3:15–17	129
5:16–21	81, 82	4:2	157
6:4–10	86		
7:6–7, 13	81	Titus 3:10	140
8–9	87		
8:9	82	Hebrews 1:13	68
8:17	81		
8:23	86, 87	1 Peter 2:2	129
10:8	89	2:23	107
11:29	105	4:17	111
11:23–12:10			
	82, 86		

INDEX BY AUTHOR AND SUBJECT

abortion 16, 19

Adams, J. 21–2, 57–60, 64n., 72–4, 93, 125–148, 154, 156f., 165f., 168

Adams, T. 35, 38n.

Anderson, R. 93, 121n.

anorexia 148

anthropology 152–4, 159

'anti-psychiatry' 126–8

arguing with God 98f., 103–5

authority 151f.

Aytoun, W. 41

Ballard, P. 26n.

Banks, R. 91n.

baptism 51, 141

Barker, M. 144n.

Barr, J. 145n.

Barrett, C. 91n.

Barth, K. 31, 57

Baxter, R. 32f., 38n., 58

Bertram, G. 92n.

Bonhoeffer, D. 41

Bosch, D. 31, 38n.

Brabham, D. 18, 25n.

Brown, C. 92n.

Browning, D. 91n.

Caird, G. 166

Calvin, J. 130

Campbell, A. 88, 91n., 92n.

Capps, D. 52, 55n., 62, 64n.

Chadwick, H. 91n.

church 132, 137f.

Clinebell, H. 8, 25n., 129

cognitive-behavioural counselling 71–5

cohabitation 125

Collins, G. 144n.

conversion 132, 139

Cotterell P. 21, 25n.

counselling 18ff., 52, 56–64, 94

covenant 110, 114–6

Crabb, L. 125, 143n., 146–156, 158, 165f., 171, 172n.

creation 68, 75, 95, 130–3, 150

cross 136f.

David 102
Deeks, D. 25n.
demons 74f.
Descartes R. 117
Dillard, A. 5
discipline 14f.
doctrine 67

Elder, J. 59, 64n.
Eliot T. S. 90
environment 134
ethics 15f.
Everton Football Club 9
exile 109–12, 115
experiential learning 10ff., 39

failure 83, 98–103
fall 130, 134f.
family therapy 134
feeling 67, 71, 132
Finney, J. 69, 76n.
forgiveness 70f., 100, 126, 143
Fowler, J. 113, 121n.
Freud, S. 60, 74, 128, 144n., 153, 156
Friedrich G. 92n.
funerals 44ff.
Furnish, V. P. 15, 91n.

Gadamer, H. 21
Gilmour, S. 79, 91n.
Gnostics 68
Goetzmann, J. 92n.
grace 130
Green, L. 11, 21–2, 25n.

groups 9, 14, 34, 39
guilt 70, 134f.

Hall, D. 91n.
Harris, T. 128
Harrison, R. 116, 121n.
hermeneutics 10, 20–23, 141, 157f.
Hiltner, S. 163
history 131
Holladay, W. 94, 121n.
Holy Spirit 24f., 30, 36f., 43, 126, 129, 151, 159, 166
homosexuality 66f.
hope 98, 112, 114, 119f., 137
hospital chaplaincy 101
human sciences 150–52
humanistic models 7f.
Hunter, R. 76n.
Hurding, R. 4, 71, 76n., 125, 143n., 156–161, 165–7

illegitimacy 51
image of God 130, 153, 159
images of ministry 88–90, 94
incarnation 29f., 96, 135f., 159
infertility 51
Isbister, N. 144n.

Jacobs, M. 57, 64n.
Jeeves, M. 144n.
Jehovah's Witnesses 14
Jeremiah 12f., 31, 93–121
Job 94, 102, 140f.
Jones, E. 144n.
judgement 97f., 114

Keck, L. 91n.
Kesey, K. 127
Kittel, G. 92n.
Kovacs, B. 121n.

Laing R. D. 127
Lake, F. 4
Lambourne, R. 4
law 94, 136, 163
leadership 95
Leonard, G. 91n.
lectionary 13, 18
liberation theology 10, 21
listening 57
Liszt, F. 117
liturgy 18
Lord's Supper 85
Lovelace, R. 158

male voice choirs 9
marriage 51, 85
Matthew 31
McGrath, A. 145n.
Meiburg, A. 25n.
mental illness 73, 128
Mills, L. 76n.
mission 15, 30–32, 37, 59, 66
Moody, D. L. 42
Mowrer, O. 72, 126–8, 131

Naomi 102
Newbigin, L. 31, 100, 121n.
Newton, J. 113
Nouwen, H. 92n.

Oates, W. 24n., 64n.
O'Donovan, O. 15, 21f., 25n.
Oglesby, W. 4, 7, 24n.
oikodomia 7f., 17, 89
Old Testament 31f., 93
Owen, J. 67, 76n.

Packer, J. 24, 38n.
parables 11, 62f.
parish audit 69
Pattison, S. 3, 4, 14, 24n.,
    25n., 80, 91n., 92n., 129,
    131, 144n.
Paul 7, 30f., 45f., 47, 72,
    79–91, 105
Perdue, L. 121n.
perfectionism 137
perspicuity of Scripture 142
Peterson, E. H. 5, 25n.
Pharisaism 41, 163
Pilate 65f.
Platonists 68
Poling, J. 10
prayer 20, 24, 60
preaching 29ff., 70, 143
proof-texting 16
prophets 94f., 96, 130, 163
Proverbs 62, 73, 94, 130, 141
Psalms 62, 94

reality 68ff.
reflection 12f., 21, 23
repentance 41, 52, 98f., 100,
    153, 160
responsibility 143
revelation 158f.

Rogers, C. 62
Ruth 102
Ryle, J. C. 33, 38n.

salvation 160
Saul 102
Saward, J. 92n.
secular counselling 59f.
sex offenders 72
sexual abuse 74f.
Shelp, E. 91, 121n.
Sibbes, R. 71, 76n.
sin 100, 130, 133–5, 153f.
singleness 51
Skinner, B. 128
Soviet Empire 74
Stott, J. 43, 55n.
success 101
suffering 98, 127, 136f.
Sutherland, R. 91n., 121n.
Szasz, T. 127

Thiselton, A. 21, 81, 91n.
Thompson, J. 121n.
Thurneysen, E. 57

Tidball, D. 88, 125, 143n.,
    162–7
training 6, 101
truth 65ff., 130, 172

Untermann, J. 121

Van Til, C. 131

Ward, P. 38n.
Westminster Pastoral
    Foundation 9
Wharton, J. 121n.
Williams, M. 21, 26n.
Willimon, W. 17, 25n., 36,
    38n.
Winter, R. 145n.
wisdom literature 94f., 115,
    130
worship 17, 35–7, 59

YMCA 9

Zephaniah 95
Zimmerli, W. 121n.